CONSTRUCTIVISM IN SCIENCE EDUCATION

CONSTRUCTIVISM IN SCIENCE EDUCATION

By

Dr. K.V. SRIDEVI

Lecturer in Education
Amrita School of Education
Amrita Vishwa Vidyapeetham
Mysore–570 026

DISCOVERY PUBLISHING HOUSE PVT. LTD.
NEW DELHI-110 002

Published by:
Namit Wasan
DISCOVERY PUBLISHING HOUSE PVT. LTD.
4383/4B, Ansari Road, Darya Ganj
New Delhi-110 002 (India)
Phone : +91-11-23279245; 23253475; 43596065
E-mail : discoverybooksindia@gmail.com
discoverypublishinghouse@gmail.com
namitwasan9@gmail.com
web : www.discoverypublishinggroup.com

***Edition:* 2020**

ISBN: 978-81-8356-345-1

Constructivism in Science Education

Printed at:
Infinity Imaging Systems
Delhi

Foreword

In the present days, improvement in the quality of school education has been a great concern of educationists, policymakers and researchers. The focus is now on to empower the child not only with desired knowledge and understandings, but also with necessary knowledge construction skills. Consequently, teachers are required to be empowered to facilitate the process of empowering children with intellectual skills for learning how to learn. Empowering children with such skills will facilitate acquisition of desired attitudes and values as well. In the context of the new millennium, major shifts in the teaching-learning process in the classroom have been emphasized. The teacher is more a facilitator of learning than an information giver, whereby the students construct knowledge by themselves through discovery and active participation in the deliberately planned activities by the teacher. Such an approach is emphasized in constructivist perspective to teaching-learning in classroom.

Constructivism is learning or meaning making theory. It suggests that individuals create their own understandings, based upon the interaction of what they already know and believe, and the phenomena or ideas with which they come into contact. It is a theory of how the learner constructs knowledge from experience, which is unique to each individual. Constructivism, according to Piaget, is a system of explanations of how learners, as individuals, adapt and refine knowledge. In this view, learners actively restructure knowledge in highly individualized ways, basing fluid intellectual configurations on existing knowledge and formal instructional experiences.

In the National Curriculum Framework of NCERT, New Delhi, formulated in 2005, a major shift is brought in the school curriculum by emphasizing constructivist approach in learning different school subjects by students at both primary and secondary levels. They have also prepared new textbooks and teacher handbooks based on constructivist principles. In-service teacher training programmes have also been conducted to enable teachers to transact the new textbooks.

Dr. Sridevi, K.V. is coming out with her first publication based on her five year long empirical study entitled "Effectiveness of Constructivist approach on students' achievement in science, scientific attitude and perception of nature of science at secondary level". The University of Mysore awarded Ph.D. Degree to her for this study in 2007. This publication is a timely contribution to the field, in line with the contemporary national level thinking at the present moment.

Dr. Sridevi, K.V. has validated in her study—Piaget's perspective on Constructivist approach in teaching of science including units from Physics, Chemistry and Biology among 8th standard students and has demonstrated its effectiveness in terms of improved students' achievement, perceptions on nature of science, scientific attitude, and science process skills. In other words, all the above effects constitute the very purposes of teaching of science at school level. The author has demonstrated the effectiveness of this new approach wherein she prepared and taught structured lessons based on constructivist principles using appropriate experimental design. She has assessed the effectiveness of this approach by using appropriate instruments developed by herself. Both the lessons and the measuring instruments are her original contributions. Although the effectiveness of constructivist approach is demonstrated in the context of science teaching, the details of how Dr. Sridevi has demonstrated practically its applicability to teach science can very well be adapted while teaching other subjects including social sciences as well. Such an adaptation can also be done, while teaching different subjects at different grade levels in secondary schools. Thus, this book can serve as a practical guide for secondary school teachers in teaching different subjects using constructivist approach.

While responding to the changes in school education at secondary level, some of the states like Kerala have already introduced this new approach to teaching in their secondary teacher education curriculum. The State has already revised textbooks at secondary school level in tune with the National Curriculum Framework (2005), emphasizing constructivist approach to teach different school subjects. This publication can be a useful guide for all the teacher trainees and teacher educators in the B.Ed colleges wherein the above innovative concepts are introduced.

I am confident that this book will also be appreciated and used by researchers in the field of school education in general and science education in particular.

The book is written in a lucid language and at the same time with technical rigour with respect to the research methodology used. The ideas are presented logically throughout, which makes reading this book useful and interesting.

I congratulate Dr. Sridevi, K.V. for this publication and her guide Dr. Manjula P Rao, Reader in Education, R.I.E., for her able guidance. I am very sure that this publication will be found useful and will receive laurels from teachers both at pre-service and in-service levels, teacher educators and researchers.

Dr. M.S. Lalitha
Professor, Department of Studies in Education
University of Mysore
Mysore

Preface

"Science is what the scientist does. It is a process by which we increase and refine our understanding and of the universe through continuous observation, experimentation, application and verification". Gagne (1965)

Learning of science in schools augments the spirit of enquiry, creativity and objectivity along with aesthetic sensibility. It aims to develop well-defined abilities of knowing, doing and being; nurtures the ability to explore and seek solution to the problems related to the environment and daily life situations and to question the existing beliefs, prejudices and practices in society. Thus, science is a must for every child to learn as it gives an opportunity to learn how to learn. The National Curriculum Framework for School Education, 2000 also viewed child as a discoverer or a scientist wherein he takes up the role of scientist and develops skills and attitudes and in turn constructs his own knowledge. Recently formulated National Curriculum Framework of 2005 has again reiterated the importance of constructivist approach emphasizing learning as a process of the construction of knowledge and learners actively construct their own knowledge by connecting new ideas to existing ideas on the basis of materials or activities presented to them. In a nutshell, they highlighted the importance of constructivist approach to teaching at all levels of school. In response to this, the NCERT have also revised textbooks on these lines and have conducted teacher training programmes for using the constructivist approach to teaching-learning in the classroom. This publication is timely and is based on the empirical study conducted in this direction. The study is entitled "Effectiveness of Constructivist approach on students' achievement in science, scientific attitude and perception of nature of science at secondary level" which was awarded Ph.D. Degree from the prestigious University of Mysore in the year 2007. The report of the same is published in the form of a book with a title, "Constructivism in Science Education".

This book is designed to make the research effort a better learning tool for student teachers, better teaching tool for teacher educators or instructors and useful reference for students working for their doctoral degree in the field of science education and the teacher educators of B.Ed. colleges.

Chapter one discusses the interrelationship between science processes and products and the synergy among the parts which makes science a whole. It presents the rationale and significance of the study taking into consideration the present status of science teaching. It gives a detailed description of Constructivism, the various faces of constructivism, difference between traditional classroom and Constructivist classroom, Constructivist learning models etc. The main objectives and hypotheses of the study formulated on the basis of philosophical, psychological and pedagogical bases of constructivism are also presented in this chapter.

Chapter two deals with the review of studies related to the present study which helped in defining the problem, formulating the objectives, conduct of the study, construction of the tools and also developed an insight into the statistical methods to be used. It gives a brief description of Philosophical and psychological insights into constructivism; characteristics of constructivist teaching and learning that helped in making decision about the type of approach to be used and how to conduct it. This chapter also presents evidences on effectiveness of constructivist approach in the field of teacher education and other subject areas and highlights the effect of Constructivist approach on outcomes of science at various levels of schooling.

Chapter three outlines the data collection procedure which is an important part of the research process, so that the hypotheses or generalizations tentatively held may be identified as valid, verified and as correct. It talks about the procedure employed to sample the population concerned, developing instructional materials, devising appropriate tools for measuring the variables like achievement test, science process skills test, scientific attitude and perception of nature of science and lastly the procedure of experimentation.

Chapter four enlightens the process of organization of quantitative data collected, in terms of editing, classifying and tabulating the information in the present study. It describes the method of analysis of the gathered data using suitable statistical techniques. Here the analysed data is interpreted for drawing conclusions and making valid generalizations. Discussion on the major findings of the study is also presented here.

Chapter five presents the gist of the whole study along with the major findings and conclusions.

I am grateful to Dr. M.S. Lalitha, learned professor of Education, Department of Studies in Education, University of Mysore, Mysore for writing a valuable foreword to this publication.

I wish to express my gratitude to my guide Dr. Manjula P. Rao, Reader in Education, Regional Institute of Education, Mysore for her valuable guidance and constant encouragement. I want to say thanks to the evaluators whose critical observations were invaluable in bringing out this book.

My grateful thanks are due to all those who have helped me for completing the study and publication of this book.

Dr. Sridevi K. V.

Contents

1

Theoretical Background of the Study

Nature of Science and Science Teaching

Science as an enterprise has individual, social, and institutional dimensions. It is fundamentally a means of understanding why things happen as they do. Man has found science as a process by which his search for answers to his unlimited questions can be approached systematically. In this way the study of science is an intellectual and social endeavour—the application of human intelligence in figuring out how the world works, should have a prominent place in any curriculum that has science literacy as one of its aims.

Bullock (1976), a historian has deemed science to be 'the greatest intellectual and cultural achievement of modern man'. He perceived science as an open-ended process in which imagination, hypotheses, criticism and controversy take a dominant role. It is not, nor was it ever, 'the closed dogmatic system of immutable laws beloved of 19th century positivists'. Bullock sees science as a humane activity, deeply concerned with man and society, providing scope for imagination and compassion as well as for observation and analysis.

Conant (1951), an eminent scientist and an educator also defined science as "an interconnected series of concepts and conceptual schemes that have developed as a result of experimentation and observation and are fruitful to further experimentation and observation".

Science thus, is simultaneously a body of knowledge and a way of gaining and using that knowledge. The accumulated and systematized body of knowledge, which is the 'product' of science—has a dynamic counterpart, the scientific attitudes and methods of inquiry-which is the 'process' of science. Science, thus is a combination of both 'processes' and 'products' related to and dependent upon each other. When, used in this way, science offers methods of inquiry useful in learning more about the universe and its workings. The interrelation and expanding nature of the processes and products of science is shown in the following figure.

Fig. 1.1: **Inter-relationship between scientific processes and products**

Source: **Carin and Sund (1964)**

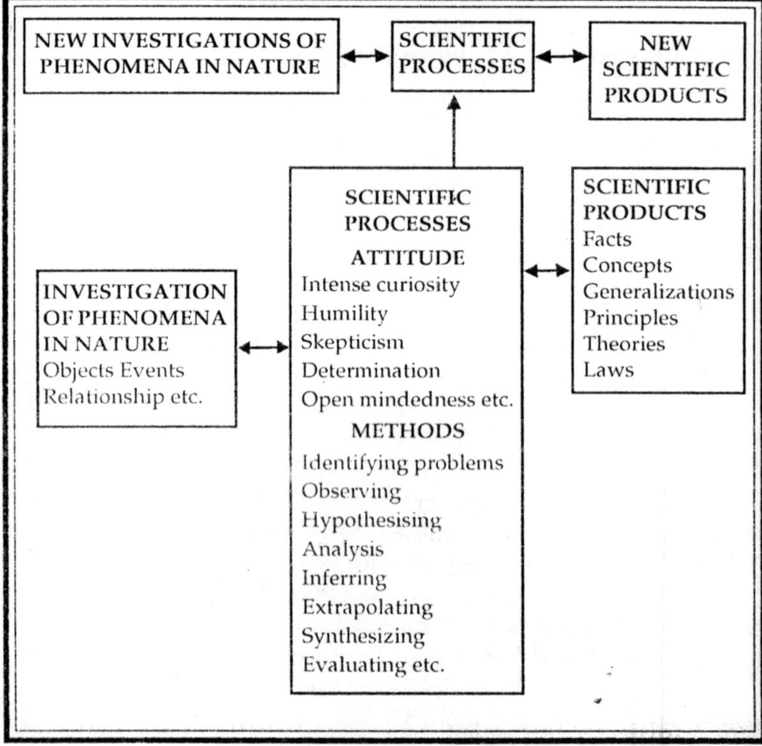

The processes of science include scientific attitudes and methods of inquiry. Scientific attitudes include both emotional attitudes such as curiosity, humility, determination and open mindedness and intellectual attitudes namely objectivity, skepticism and rationality. The methods of inquiry are observing, hypothesizing, analyzing, inferring, extrapolating, reasoning, synthesizing etc. The scientific attitudes develop simultaneously with science process skill development and with the discovery or construction of useful science ideas. The information and ideas of science that compose its knowledge base are often referred to as 'products' since new discoveries add to the base of scientific information which are the products of curiosity and experimentation. An interesting thing about science knowledge is that new discoveries often lead to more questions, more experiments, and further discoveries. The science cycle move under its own momentum, propelled initially and again later sustained by human curiosity and a desire to explain natural phenomena. The effect is an exploding accumulation of new information that is added to the knowledge base. Scientific knowledge consists of primarily facts, concepts, principles and theories. The scientific theories are refined in the light of new ideas which Kuhn (1970) called a new paradigm.

Fig. 1.2: **The science cycle**

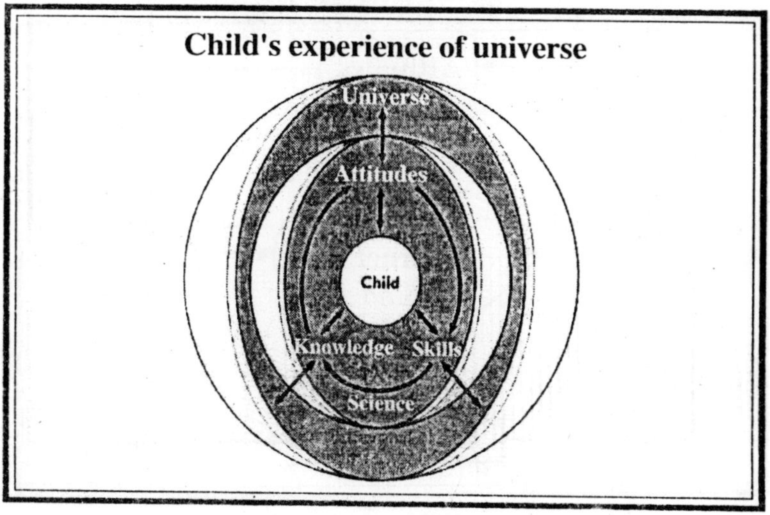

Child's experience of universe

Universe
Attitudes
Child
Knowledge
Skills
Science

It is a well-known fact that children are curious. Their curiosity motivates them to discover new ways to use this powerful key for unlocking the mysteries of their world. As said earlier, both the products and processes for acquiring them are to be experienced by the students. Children receive a whole science experience when they are immersed in all the three parts of science. The synergy among the parts which makes science whole is shown in the Science cycle given in fig. 1.2.

Attitudes are mental predispositions towards people, objects, events and so on. In science, attitudes are important because of three primary factors. First, a child's attitude carries a mental state of readiness with it. With a positive attitude the child will perceive science objects, topics, activities and people positively. Secondly, attitudes are not innate or inborn. They are learned and organized through experiences as children develop. Thirdly, attitudes are dynamic result of experiences that act as directive factors when a child enters into new experiences. As a result, attitudes carry an emotional as well as an intellectual tone. Attitudes not only improve achievement, but also build up interest and self esteem which is represented in the following diagram.

Fig. 1.3: **Importance of basic science attitudes**

Source: **Adapted from Benjamin Bloom, Human characteristics and school learning (New York: McGraw-Hill, 1979)**

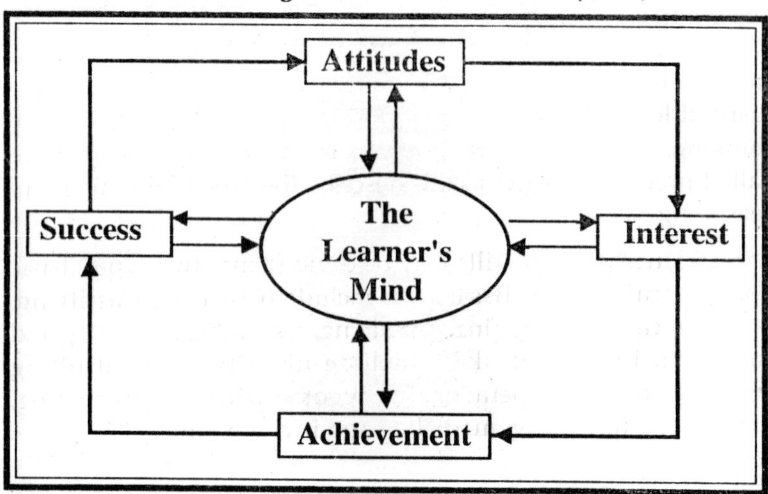

It is essential to distinguish between the two broad subsets of science related attitudes. Attitude towards science, according to Duckworth (1975) refers to the "disposition of mind for or against scientists, scientific activity and learning of science" and has predominantly affective orientation. On the other hand, scientific attitude is "the cognitive attitude or belief about thinking and has also affective and behavioural aspects"(Guilford, 1978). Grinell had listed down around 20 scientific attitudes namely; empiricism, determinism, a belief that problems have solutions, parsimony, scientific manipulation, skepticism, precision, respect for paradigm, a respect for power of theoretical structure, willingness to change opinion, loyalty to reality, aversion to superstition and an automatic preference for scientific explanation, a thirst for knowledge, an "intellectual drive", suspended judgment, awareness of assumptions, ability to separate fundamental concepts from the irrelevant or unimportant, respect for quantification and appreciation of mathematics, an appreciation of probability and statistics, an understanding that knowledge has tolerance limit and empathy for the human condition.

Apart from the knowledge and attitudes, there is one more part of science i.e. science process skills. Children learn how to learn by thinking critically and using information creatively. They continue to learn how to learn when making discriminating observations, when organizing and analysing facts and concepts, when giving reasons for expected outcomes, when evaluating and interpreting the results of experiments and when drawing justifiable conclusions (Victor, 1971). In science, the ways of thinking, measuring, solving problems and using thoughts are called processes. Process skills describe the type of thinking and reasoning required.

Science process skills may be divided into two types: basic and integrated skills. Basic skills include observing, classifying, communicating, measuring, estimating, reasoning, predicting and inferring. Integrated skills include identifying, controlling variables, defining operationally, hypothesizing, experimenting, graphing, interpreting, modelling and investigating.

Science process skills along with science related attitudes lead to discovery of scientific knowledge that is the product side of science. Scientific knowledge is tentative. A scientific finding or a prediction, which is accepted to be true at a particular time, is probabilistic and not absolute. It is derived from imagination, observation and experimentation. Scientific knowledge is rational and empirical i.e. it has its origin in the real world, and dependent on sense experiences. It is holistic; the knowledge gathered by various branches of science contribute to an overall conceptual scheme or mental construct , which is internally consistent. As a product of creative human imagination, concepts of science reflect the social and cultural background of their times.

The values that underlie science represent the very human origin itself. It can be argued that without these values, the enterprise of science could not have occurred. They are,

- Consideration of consequences—decision based on the assessment of the effects emanating from an action or a set of actions.
- Longing to know and understand.
- Demand for verification—search for supporting evidence to verify the validity and accuracy of a statement.
- Questioning—belief that all things, including "self-evident" truths are open to question.
- Respect for logic—consideration of influences that emerge from cause-effect relationships.
- Search for data and their meanings.

Why teach science in school? or more importantly—Why should young people at school attempt to learn it? There are a number of responses to these questions. Association for Science Education (ASE, 1981) gave explanations to these questions, as science is both deeply interesting and beautiful in construction. The pursuit of knowledge in science is an end in itself, an intellectual activity leading to the creation of further research and knowledge. Science is a part of the world of ideas; its history, philosophy, literature, pedagogy and social institutions contribute to the culture of our societies. Science has high utilitarian value. High achievement in science can lead to a wide range of life chances, active participation in the process of democratic decision-making, understanding how some principles and laws in science can provide a basis for rational choice in life contexts.

Learning of science in schools augment the spirit of enquiry, creativity and objectivity along with aesthetic sensibility. It aims to develop well-defined abilities of knowing, doing and being. It also nurtures the ability to explore and seek solution of the problems related to the environment and daily life situations and to question the existing beliefs, prejudices and practices in society. Thus science is must for every child to learn as it gives an opportunity to learn how to learn. In India the inclusion of science as a discipline and improvement in the science education is the successful effort of various committees and commissions.

One of the oldest commissions, University Education Commission (1948) felt that improvement of curriculum and syllabus at the secondary level is essential for the improvement of University Education and recommended the inclusion of science as a discipline at secondary level. Later, Secondary Education Commission (1953) suggested compulsory inclusion of general science and mathematics as core subjects at the middle school as well as secondary level. Then, the Indian Education Commission (1964-66) identified the need of a revolution in the educational system through internal transformation by relating it to the life needs and aspirations of the nation, by achieving qualitative improvement, by expanding educational facilities and by relating education to productivity and recommended science as an integral part of education. Science teaching was 'to promote an ever deepening understanding of basic principles; to develop problem solving and analytical skills; to inculcate ability to apply them to the problems of the natural environment and social living and to promote the spirit of inquiry and experimentation'. Overall, it heralded a major shift in the school science policy from a general science approach to structure of discipline approach.

During the period 1967-72, efforts were mounted to implement the recommendations of UNESCO Planning

Commission (1964) and Education Commission (1964-66). Besides this, The Planning Group Education (1968) gave high priority to the development of science education by laying emphasis on the development of scientific attitudes and skills. In 1972, a variety of materials such as Physical Science Study Committee (PSSC), Biological Science Study Committee (BSSC), School Mathematics Study Group (SMSG) and Chemical Bond Approach (CBA) etc. were produced. Again, the period 1972-77 was a watershed for the school science education policy in our country. Entirely new approaches of teaching science emerged in schools.

Considerable effort was made at national level by NCERT (1961) to improve the quality of science education. Revision of the science curriculum, providing in-service training for science teachers on the new approaches of teaching and evaluation were the major focused areas. According to the 42nd amendment of the Constitution of India—Part IVA fundamental duties of citizen 51A(h), it shall be the duty of every citizen of India to develop the scientific temper, humanism and the spirit of enquiry and reform (1976).

Based on the recommendations given by the above committees and commissions, the following main objectives of science teaching were arrived for secondary schools.

The teaching of science at secondary level should aim at acquisition of:

- knowledge of fundamental principles and concepts useful in daily life.
- skills of experimentation, construction, observation, drawing and problem solving and invention.
- abilities in the students such as ability to sense a problem, to organize, interpret, analyse, generalize, predict from given data, organize science exhibition, fairs etc.
- inculcating interest in the environment they live in.
- scientific attitudes like critical thinking, open-mindedness, curiosity, objectivity, free from

superstitions and false beliefs, willingness to suspend judgments, belief in cause and effect relationship, rationality etc., and interests.

- a broad genuine appreciation of what development of science means to modern, social, industrial and national life and preparing the students for better living i.e. forming basis for vocational career.
- train the students for reflective thinking.

Constructivism and Science Teaching

Tracing the schools of learning, one would see how there had been a different gamut of ideas and origin of developmental schools resulted in behaviourism and cognitivism. Behaviourism, which associates learning to response strengthening, whereby the learner is repeatedly cued to give a simple response followed by immediate feedback and passively receives rewards and punishment, is simply becoming irrelevant. Cognitivism associates learning to knowledge acquisition and considers information as a commodity that can be transmitted directly from teacher to learner may retain some relevance but is not enough. This is constructivist era. Constructivism associates learning to the building of one's own knowledge, is much more appropriate to today's situation, in that it views learning in the perspective of the learner. The teacher is considered as a cognitive guide while the learner is empowered to construct his own meaning, not just memorize the right answers.

Constructivism is not a new concept. It is a learning or meaning making theory. It suggests that individuals create their own understandings, based upon the interaction of what they already know and believe and the phenomena or ideas with which they come into contact. Constructivism is a descriptive theory of learning not a prescriptive theory of learning. It has its roots in philosophy and has been applied to sociology and anthropology, as well as cognitive psychology and education. Perhaps the first constructivist philosopher, Giambatista Vico commented in a treatise in 1710 that "one only knows something if one can explain it" (Yager, 1991). Constructivism is a theory of how the learner constructs knowledge from experience, which is unique to each individual. Duckworth (1987) defined constructivism succinctly:

"Meaning is not given to us in our encounters, but it is given by us, constructed by us, each in our own way, according to how our understanding is currently organized".

Crowther (1997), defined constructivism as "Constructivism means that as we experience something new, we internalize it through our past experiences or knowledge constructs we have previously established." Constructivism bristles with philosophical questions: it explicitly assumes positions in the philosophy of science, the philosophy of mind, and the philosophy of education. It is at once a theory of science, of human learning and of teaching.

Constructivism according to Piaget (1971) is a system of explanations of how learners as individuals adapt and refine knowledge. In this view, learners actively restructure knowledge in highly individualized ways, basing fluid intellectual configurations on existing knowledge and formal instructional experiences.

Most constructivists would agree that the traditional approach to teaching-the transmission model—promotes neither the interaction between prior and new knowledge nor the conversations that are necessary for internalization and deep understanding. The information required from traditional teaching if acquired at all, is usually not integrated with other knowledge held by the students. Thus new knowledge is often only brought forth for school like activities such as examinations and ignored as all other times.

Among the constructivists, there are those who focus on the individual acting as sole agent in the process of constructing and reconstructing meaning. Others focus on the socio-cultural context in which an individual live and still others focussed on both the individual and social context by suggesting that it is not useful to separate the two analytically.

Faces of Constructivism

The various faces of constructivism are as follows:

(i) Trivial Constructivism

This is the simplest idea in constructivism what Glaserfeld (1990) calls trivial constructivism also known as personal constructivism. The principle has been credited to Piaget, pioneer of constructivist thought and can be summed up by the following statement:

"Knowledge is, actively constructed by the learner, not passively received from the environment". This reacts against other epistemologies promoting simplistic model of communication as simple transmission of meanings from one person to another. The prior knowledge of the learner is essential to be able to "actively" construct new knowledge.

(ii) Radical Constructivism

It adds a second principle to trivial constructivism, which can be expressed as: "Coming to know is a process of dynamic adaptation towards viable interpretations of experience. The knower does not necessarily construct knowledge of a "real" "world".

Radical constructivism challenges the notion of external reality; no amount of stimuli, experience, or thinking is sufficient to prove the existence of an external agent. Radical constructivism does not deny an objective reality but simply states that we have no way of knowing what that reality might be. Mental constructs, constructed from past experience help to impose order on one's flow of continuing experience. However, when they fail to work because of external or internal constraints, thus causing problem, the constructs change to try and accommodate the new experience. Within the constraints that limit our construction, there is room for infinity of alternatives. From a radical constructivist perspective, communication need not involve identically shared meanings between participants. It is sufficient for their meanings to be compatible (Hardy and Taylor, 1997). The emphasis here is still clearly on the individual learner as a constructor. Neither trivial nor radical constructivism looks closely at the extent to which the human environment affects learning. These issues are focused on in more detail by social, cultural and critical constructivism.

(iii) Social Constructivism

The social world of a learner includes the people that directly affect that person—teachers, friends, students, administrators and participants in all forms of activity. This takes into account the social nature of both the local processes in collaborative learning and in the discussion of wider social collaboration in a given subject, such as science.

Vygotsky (1978), a pioneering theorist in psychology focused on the roles that society play in the development of an individual. He believed everything is learned on two levels—first, through interaction with others and then integrated into the individual's mental structure. A more experienced partner is able to provide "scaffolding" of the subject matter to support the student's evolving understanding. Another aspect of Vygotsky's theory is the idea that the potential for cognitive development is limited to a "Zone of proximal development". This zone is the area of exploration for which the student is cognitively prepared but requires help and social interaction to fully develop. Cobb (1994) followed by Salomon and Perkins (1998) suggested that "acquisition" and "participation" the two metaphors of learning interrelate and interact in synergistic ways.

Teaching strategies using social constructivism as a referent include teaching in contexts that might be personally meaningful to students, negotiating taken-as-shared, meanings with students, class discussions, small-group collaboration, and valuing meaningful activity over correct answers (Wood et al., 1995).

(iv) Cultural Constructivism

Beyond the immediate social environment of a learning situation are the wider context of cultural influences including custom, religion, biology, tools and language. For example, the format of books can affect learning, by promoting views about the organization, accessibility and status of the information they contain.

"(What we need) is a new conception of the mind, not as an individual information processor, but as a biological, developing system that exists equally well within an individual brain and in the tools, artifacts, and symbolic systems used to facilitate social and cultural interaction" (Vosniadou, 1996).

The tools that we use, affect the way we think (by tools including language and other symbolic systems as well as physical tools). Salomon and Perkins (1998) identified two effects of tools on the learning mind. Firstly, they redistribute the cognitive load between people and the tool while being used and secondly, the use of tool can affect the mind beyond actual use, by changing skills, perspectives and ways of representing the world. For example, computers carry an entire philosophy of knowledge construction, symbol manipulation, design and exploration, which if used in schools can subversively promote changes in curricula, assessment, and other changes in teaching and learning.

Higher mental functions are, by definition, culturally mediated. They involve not a direct action on the world but an indirect one; that takes a bit of material matter used previously and incorporates it as an aspect of action. So far as that matter itself has been shaped by prior human practice, current action incorporated the mental work that produced in the particular form of that matter (Cole and Wertsch, 1996).

(v) Critical Constructivism

Critical constructivism looks at constructivism within a social and cultural environment, but adds a critical dimension aimed at reforming these environments in order to improve the success of constructivism applied as referent.

Taylor (1996) describes critical constructivism as a social epistemology that addresses the socio-cultural context of knowledge construction and serves as a referent for cultural reform. Critical constructivism adds a greater emphasis on actions for change of learning teacher. It is a framework using the critical theory of Habermas to help make potentially disempowering cultural myths more visible and hence more open to questions through conversation and critical self-reflection. An important part of that framework is the promotion of communicative ethics that is conditions for establishing dialogues oriented towards achieving mutual understanding (Taylor, 1998). The conditions include: a primary concern for maintaining empathetic, caring and trusting relationships; a commitment to dialogue that aims to achieve reciprocal understanding of goals, interests and standards; and concern for and critical awareness of the often-invisible rules of the classroom, including social and cultural myths. Together these myths produce a culture that portrays classroom teaching and learning as "a journey through a pre-constructed landscape". Modification of such entrenched environments to reduce myths and promote approaches based on constructivism is problematic; because of the self-reinforcing mature of administration and the effects of wider culture.

(vi) Psychological Constructivism

Psychological constructivism is based on Jean Piaget's model of development of the individual. The process focuses learning as a personal, individual, intellectual construction based on experiences of one in the world. To Piaget, the child's mind is self-organized by a constant antagonism between internal, subjective mental states and external reality. In Piagetian theory, there is no objective ontological reality. For Piaget (1952, 1969) the development of human intellect proceeds through adaptation and organization. Adaptation is a process of assimilation and accommodation, where, on one hand, external events are assimilated into thoughts and on the other, new and unusual mental structures are accommodated into the mental environment. The process of organization refers to the structuring of the adapted mental material. Piaget considers that the organization of the mind is accomplished through a series of increasingly complex and integrated ways, of which the simplest one is scheme, i.e. a mental representation of some action that can be performed on an object. As Piaget identifies knowledge with action, he considers that mental development organizes these schemes in more complex and integrated ways to produce the adult mind. This progression occurs because of the reciprocal effects of assimilation and accommodation constantly forced to attain equilibrium between subjective and objective states.

Fig. 1.4: **Construction of Knowledge.**

Source: **Adapted from Appleton. (1993) "Using theory to guide practice: Teaching science from a constructivist perspective"**

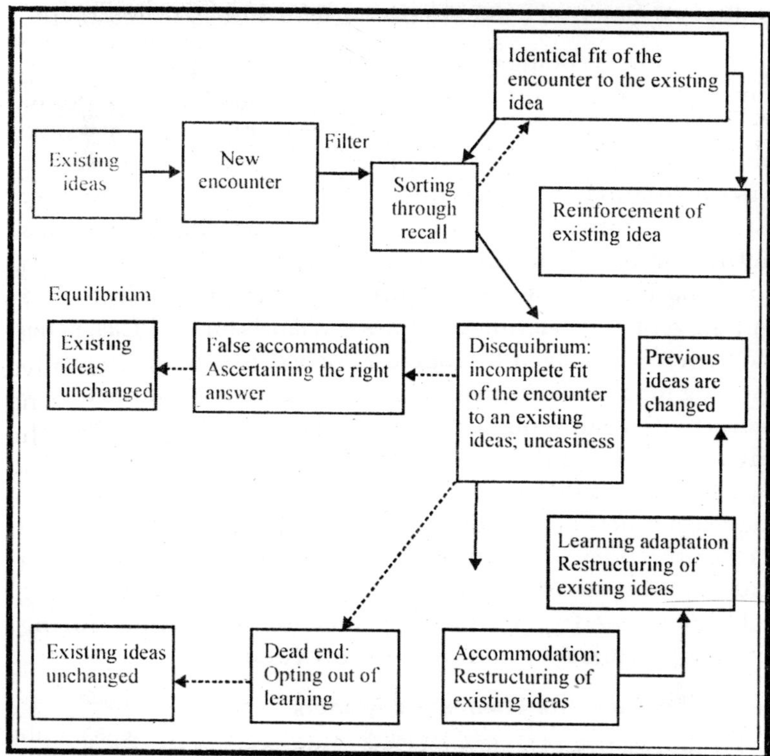

Piaget assumed that there exists four major periods of development in the evolution of human mind: The sensorimotor period (from birth to two) where in the child explores the world through action. This period is subdivided into pre-conceptual and the intuitive period. The pre-conceptual child (age 2 to 4) does not have fully developed concepts and the ability to abstract and discriminate relevant features. The child cannot appropriately use inductive and deductive ways of thinking. The intuitive child (age 4 to 7) forms ideas just from impressions and the child cannot consider more than one variable at once. In the concrete operational period (age 7 to 11), the child can manipulate numbers, develop concept formation skills and think hypothetically about coordinated action, where two or more variables can be considered at once. In the formal operational period (adolescence and adulthood), the child will have the capacity of abstract reasoning.

Learning by doing and forming ideas from exploration is the underlying theory behind psychological constructivism. The child is viewed like a scientist who possesses insights, questions, problem solving strategies and new ideas that will be used in experimentation. The scientific process of puzzling, probing, testing are incorporated into the approach. The child develops his picture or understanding of the physical world through manipulation and seeing relationships between objects and learning centrally determined names and labels for the ideas, items and activities involved through experience. Key to the theory is fostering independence in the child, not dependence on adults so that, activities, curriculum, environment are based on risk-taking, self-direction, guided or totally free discovery type, experimentation through social interaction and problem solving. The teacher acts as a facilitator of the educational context. The teacher provides opportunities for observation, interaction of students with each other and with the teacher through questioning techniques, modifying the environment, supporting during conflicts and planning and creating curriculum.

Constructivism—Its Theory and Models

Constructivism is anchored on cognitive psychology but from a practical perspective has roots in the "progressive" model of John Dewey (1933). According to this theory, learners are active participants in knowledge acquisition and engage in restructuring, manipulating, reinventing, and experimenting with knowledge to make it meaningful, organized and permanent. Learning is an internal process influenced by the learner's personality, prior knowledge and learning goals (Davidson, 1995).

Constructivism describes a learner-centered environment where knowledge and the making of knowledge is interactive, inductive and collaborative, where multiple perspectives are represented, and where questions are valued (Brooks and Brooks, 1993; Brown, Collins and Duguid, 1989; Lebow, 1993) and the importance of context related to knowledge and learning is emphasized. That is knowing and the process of learning are affected by the context of the learning environment and are referred to as "situated cognition" (Brown, Collins and Duguid, 1989). In addition, within the constructivist environment the importance of "authentic activity" (Brown, et al., Lebow, 1993) is emphasized as a part of the learning process.

Lerman (1989) following Kilpatrick (1987) suggested that the core epistemological theses of constructivism are

'Knowledge is actively constructed by the cognizing subject, not passively received from the environment'. 'Coming to know is an adaptive process that organizes one's experiential world; it does not discover an independent, pre-existing world outside the mind of the knower'.

First point is a psychological claim and second the epistemological claim. Wheatley (1991) offers a nearly identical summation of the epistemological core of constructivism. He said

"The theory of constructivism rests on the two main principles....principle one states that knowledge is not passively received, but is actively built up by the cognizing subject.... Principle two states that the function of cognition is adaptive and serves the organization of the experiential world not the discovery of ontological reality.... Thus we do not find truth but construct viable explanations of our experiences."

Scott (1987) defines a constructivist in science as one who "perceives students as active learners who come to science lessons already holding ideas about natural phenomena, which they use, make sense of everyday experiences. .... Such a process is one in which learners actively make sense of the world by constructing meaning."

For Piaget, action rather than language is the basis of all knowledge. His theory describes the gradual evolution of thought in logical terms from stage to stage, which are also hierarchically determined. Vygotsky goes a step further saying "Instruction precedes development". He, therefore, analysed intellectual development as a function of instruction...Concepts do not exist in isolation. Vygotsky had a firm belief i.e. belief in the social construction of the mind. Within the context of cultural development, any function in the child appears twice, namely social plane and psychological plane. The language plays the mediating role and Vygotsky thus, talked of the tools of language. He had a bold conception in the "Zone of proximal development" whereby individual activity is detached from communal practice. Jerome Bruner (1966) unlike Piaget believed in symbolic growth. He informed about what ought to be the plan of attack unlike Piaget who talked of the universal child. Bruner stressed the role of language and culture in education of children so that the children learn "how to learn". Along with Piaget and Bruner, Ausubel (1978) was also a strong advocate of meaningful learner. He saw the importance of meaning as a key factor for learning.

From the above theories, constructivists have evolved the following models and approaches.

There are several **constructivist design models** available.

(i) The learning cycle is a three-step design that can be used as a general framework for many kinds of constructivist activities. The process begins with the "discovery" phase. In it, the teacher encourages students to generate questions and hypotheses from working with various materials. Next, the teacher provides "concept introduction" lessons. Here, the teacher focuses on the students' questions and helps them create hypotheses and design experiments. In the third step, "concept application" students work on new problems that reconsider the concepts studied in the first two steps. The cycle continues again.

(ii) The Biological Science Curriculum Study (BSCS) developed an instructional model for constructivism which was called the "Five Es" by Roger Bybee. In these models the process is explained by employing five "E"s. They are: Engage, Explore, Explain, Elaborate and Evaluate.

(iii) Gagnon and Collay developed another constructivist learning design. In this model, teachers implement number of steps in their teaching structure. They develop a situation for students to explain; select a process for groupings of materials and students; build a bridge between what students already know and what teachers want them to learn; anticipate questions to ask and answer without giving away an explanation; encourage students to exhibit a record of their thinking by sharing it with others and solicit students' reflections about their learning.

(iv) Mc. Clintock and Black (1995) derived a model from several computer technology-supported learning environments. The Information Construction (ICON) model contains seven stages: a. Observation: Students make observations of primary source materials embedded in their natural context or simulations thereof. b. Interpretation Construction: Students interpret their observations and explain their reasoning. c. Contextualisation: Students construct contexts for their explanations. d. Cognitive Apprenticeship: Teachers help student apprentices' master observation, interpretation and contextualization. e. Collaboration: Students collaborate in observation, interpretation and contextualization. f. Multiple Interpretations: Students gain cognitive flexibility by being exposed to multiple interpretations from other students and from expert examples. g. Multiple Manifestations: Students gain transferability by seeing multiple manifestations of the same interpretations.

(v) Planning and Learning Cycle. 4E's Model

The four E's indicate exploration, explanation, expansion and evaluation. In the first stage, Explore, the students first encounter and identify the instructional task. Here, they make connections between past and present learning experiences. Lay the organizational ground work for the activities ahead and stimulate their involvement in the anticipation of these activities. The students have the opportunity to get directly involved with phenomena and materials. Involving themselves in the activities along with others, students build a base of common experience, which assist them in the process of sharing and communicating. The student observes, identifies, classifies in this phase.

In the second stage, Explain, is the point at which the learner begins to put the abstract experience through which he or she has gone into a communicable form. Communication occurs between peers, the facilitator or within the learner himself.

In the stage three, Expand, the students expand on the concepts they have learned, make connections to other related concepts and apply their understandings to the world around them.

And lastly, Evaluate, the fourth "E", is an ongoing diagnostic process that allows the teacher to determine if the learner has attained understanding of the concepts and knowledge. Evaluation and assessment can occur at all points along the continuum of the instructional process.

This model is simple, thorough, convenient and conducive to use in the classroom and has considerable potential to have an effect on the improvement in students' learning. It is not only a planning model but also a teaching model. This Constructivist model closely follows the original format of the Science Curriculum Improvement Study (SCIS), which is credited with the greatest student achievement gains in major research studies and significant improvements in student science and their attitudes and inquiry skills when compared to similar experimental science programs and traditional science curricula (Shymansky et al., 1982; Bredderman, 1982).

Role of Constructivist Approach in Science Classroom

A constructivist learning setting differs from the one based on the traditional model. In a constructivist classroom, learning outcomes not only depend on the learning environment but also on the knowledge of the learner. Learning involves the construction of meanings by students from what they see or hear may or may not be those intended. It is a continuous and an active process, which is influenced to a large extent by existing knowledge. Firstly, current ideas of pupils are elicited using several strategies. These include pupils writing, expressing orally, card-sorting exercises, presenting pupils with description of events and asking them to decide whether they are true or false, pupils producing posters on a particular idea. In this regard, Driver et. al. (1994) identified five possible forms, depending on the outcome of the elicitation phase. These are:

- Developing existing ideas (if no misunderstandings are apparent);
- Differentiating between existing ideas (where two or more scientific ideas may be seen as one by pupils, e.g. dissolving and melting);
- Integrating existing ideas (where pupils may hold several ideas relating to one scientific idea);
- Changing existing ideas (where pupils hold ideas which differ from the scientifically accepted ideas); and
- Introducing new ideas

After elicitation phase, the most difficult thing is changing existing ideas. Among the various methods, the most prominent ones are socratic questioning and introducing discrepant event in order to induce cognitive conflict, disequilibrium or dissonance in the minds of pupils. These approaches will help in the modification of existing ideas and in construction of new ideas. After the evaluation of the ideas, they are applied in new situations. Later, the new idea is compared with previous ideas. Thus, meanings, once constructed, are evaluated and can be accepted or rejected. Learners take the final responsibility of their learning (Driver and Bell, 1986). The process of construction of new ideas is shown in the fig. 1.5.

During the process of learning the students actively participate in various activities both individual and group work; share their feelings and ideas, reconstruct the meanings whenever required. There is no single approach or strategy used in a constructivist classroom, it is an eclectic approach made use of with a variety of methods, strategies and techniques but following the principles of constructivist approach. During the process of construction of meanings, the students make use of various process skills and develop positive attitudes. There is every chance provided to practice and understand the nature of science and inculcate scientific attitude among the students.

Fig. 1.5: **The constructivist teaching model developed by the children's learning in science project team.**

Source: Driver and Oldham (1986).

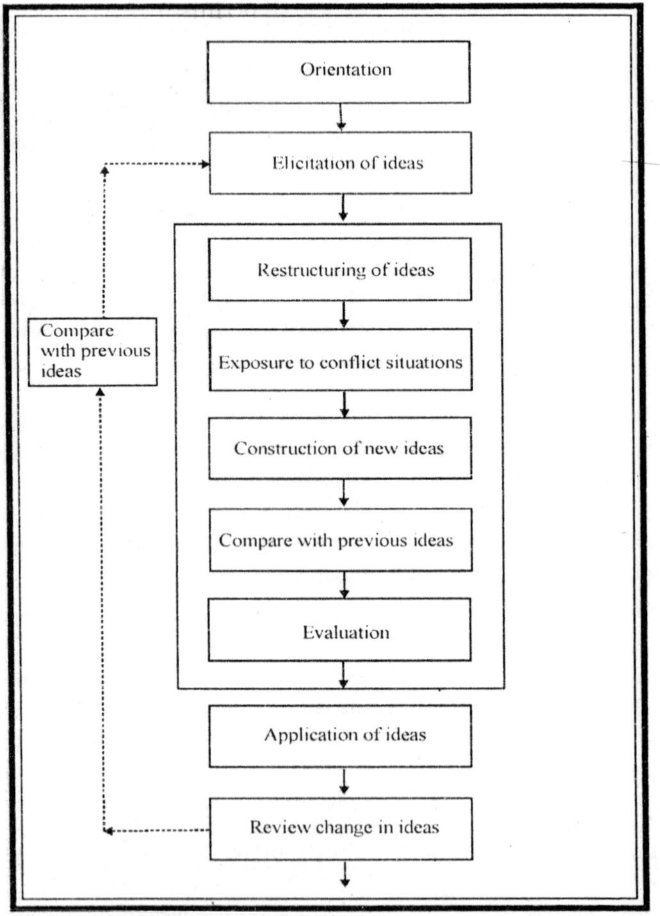

Various educators and cognitive psychologists have applied constructivism to the development of learning environments.

Jonassen (1991) isolated a number of design principles:

- Create real-world environments that employ the context in which learning is relevant;

- Focus on realistic approaches to solve real-world problems;
- The instructor is a coach and analyzer of the strategies used to solve these problems;
- Stress conceptual interrelatedness, providing multiple representations or perspectives on the content;
- Instructional goals and objectives should be negotiated and not imposed;
- Evaluation should serve as a self-analysis tool;
- Provide tools and environments that help learners interpret the multiple perspectives of the world;
- Learning should be internally controlled and mediated by the learner.

Wilson and Cole (1991) provide a description of cognitive teaching models, which "embody" constructivist concepts. The following concepts central to constructivist design, teaching and learning were isolated:

- Embed learning in a rich authentic problem-solving environment;
- Provide for authentic versus academic contexts for learning;
- Provide for learner control;
- Use errors as a mechanism to provide feedback on learner's understanding.

Brooks et al. (1993) gave the following suggestions for constructivist classroom:

- Student autonomy and initiative are accepted and encouraged.
- The teacher asks open-ended questions and allows wait time for responses.
- Higher-level thinking is encouraged.

- Students are engaged in a dialogue with the teacher and with each other.
- Students are engaged in experiences that challenge hypotheses and encourage discussion.
- The class uses raw data, primary sources, and manipulative, physical and interactive materials.
- The goal of the learner is to regurgitate the accepted explanation or methodology expostulated by the teacher.

Brooks and Brooks (1993) offered an interesting comparison of the visible differences between "traditional" classroom and "constructivist" classrooms. Their comparison is as follows:

- Students primarily work in groups unlike individually as in traditional classroom.
- Curriculum is presented whole to part with emphasis on the big concept whereas in traditional classroom it is vice versa.
- Pursuit of student questions is highly valued whereas in traditional classroom strict adherence to a fixed curriculum is valued.
- Curricular activities rely heavily on primary resources unlike relying only on textbooks.
- Students are viewed as thinkers with emerging theories about the world (Cognitive apprentices) unlike its counterpart.
- Teachers are information dispensers and assess only to validate student lessons in traditional classroom where as a constructivist teacher generally behave in interactive manner mediating the environment for students and seeks student's point of view in order to understand student learning for use in subsequent conceptions.

Jonassen (1993) summarizes the following principles illustrating how knowledge construction can be facilitated:

- Provide multiple representations of reality;
- Represent the natural complexity of the real-world;
- Focus on knowledge construction, not reproduction;
- Present authentic tasks;
- Provide real-world, case-based learning environments, rather than predetermined instructional sequences;
- Foster reflective practice;
- Enable context and content dependent knowledge construction;
- Support collaborative construction of knowledge through social negotiation.

Ernest (1995) in his description of the many schools of thought of constructivism suggests the following implications of constructivism which derive from both the radical and social perspectives:

- Sensitivity toward and attentiveness to the learner's previous constructions;
- Diagnostic teaching attempting to remedy learner's errors and misconceptions;
- Attention to metacognition and strategic self-regulation by learners;
- The use of multiple representations of mathematical concepts;
- Awareness of the importance of goals for the learner, and the dichotomy between learner and teacher goals;
- Awareness of the importance of social contexts, such as the difference between folk or street mathematics and school mathematics.

Honebein (1996) describes seven goals for the design of constructivist learning environments:

- Provide experience with the knowledge construction process;

- Provide experience in and appreciation for multiple perspectives;
- Embed learning in realistic and relevant contexts;
- Encourage ownership and voice in the learning process;
- Embed learning in social experience;
- Encourage the use of multiple modes of representation,
- Encourage self-awareness in the knowledge construction process.

It is understood from the above description that, constructivism unlike the conventional method of teaching involves exploration of students' preexisting ideas and their construction or reconstruction accordingly using various child centered strategies of teaching. The student autonomy and initiative are accepted and encouraged in the classroom. Thus, this innovative approach will result not only in developing cognitive abilities but also to modify attitudes, increase self-confidence and decision making ability among the students.

Role of Teacher in a Constructivist Classroom

In the constructivist classroom, the role of teacher also demands new orientation to suit the modern temper and times. Almost all students in one way or another construct their own meanings while acquiring knowledge. It is a very valuable mental activity of pupils, which should not be ignored thoughtlessly. It is then up to the pupils to link and interlink concepts by developing strategies to help themselves in construction of their new knowledge. This in other words, means that knowledge is constructed and reconstructed progressively in the presence of the teacher.

The teacher becomes a guide for the learner, providing bridging or scaffolding, helping to extend the learner's zone of proximal development. The student is encouraged to develop metacognitive skills such as reflective thinking and problem solving techniques. The independent learner is intrinsically motivated to generate, discover, build and enlarge her/his own framework of knowledge. The teacher is a facilitator or coach in the constructivist learning approach. The teacher guides the student, stimulating and provoking the student's critical thinking, analysing and synthesising throughout the learning process. The teacher is also a co-learner.

More emphasis is on organizing and meaningful learning than mechanical learning, emphasis on improvement of thinking than the attainment of narrowly conceived specific understandings and skills will be laid by the teacher. Right concept formation, application of scientific knowledge to unknown situation, designing and executing varied problem solving procedures are encouraged in the learning process. Over all, a swing towards self-study, self-understanding and self-education among students rather than authoritarian or dominated teaching learning process by teachers is found in a constructivist classroom.

From the above discussion, it is clear that in constructivist approach of science learning, the students are given utmost freedom and ownership to what they learn and the role of the teacher is to provide such experiences that give them an opportunity to construct knowledge. In this process, students make use of science processes to construct knowledge, resulting in not only learning of concepts but also a better understanding of nature of science and favourable science attitudes were developed among the students.

Rationale and Significance of the Study

The aims and objectives of science education at secondary level spelt out were unfortunately not implemented properly. In spite of the effort made by many committees and commissions as listed earlier, the quality of science education is not satisfactory. After the District primary education project intervention programme, there is a change in the textbooks, role of the teacher, involvement of community and so on. The textbooks are activity based, inclusion of learner-centered teaching learning process and increased utilization of community resources. But still, the change is not up to the mark. In this connection, both at international and national level, changes were emphasized in the teaching and learning process and also in content standards. The National Science Education Standards (1996) emphasized the following changes in teaching and content standards laying more emphasis on:

- Understanding and responding to individual student's interests, strengths, experiences and needs.
- Focusing on student understanding and use of scientific knowledge, ideas and inquiry processes.
- Guiding students in active and extended scientific inquiry.
- Providing opportunities for scientific discussion and debate among students and continuously assessing student understanding.
- Supporting a classroom community with cooperation, shared responsibility and respect.
- Understanding scientific concepts and developing abilities of inquiry.
- Learning subject matter disciplines in the context of inquiry, technology, science in personal and social perspectives and history and nature of science.
- Integrating all aspects of science content.
- Implementing inquiry as instructional strategies, abilities and ideas to be learned.

At national level, National Curriculum Framework for School Education, 2000 brought out by the National Council of Educational Research and Training (NCERT) emphasized viewing the child as a constructor of knowledge. Learning of science up to secondary stage needs to be replaced by learning of science and technology in view of strong organic linkages between the two. It also recommended the following:

- Scientific attitudes and skills should be developed.
- Students are needed to be exposed to the nature and structure of science and the support it provides to the technological developments.
- Learning of science would be built around natural and social elements of environment.

- Focus would be on understanding of concepts and applications in the areas of matter and its properties, energy, relationship of various physical processes and the technological applications of principles of science.
- Science, technology, society and environment would coalesce in teaching and learning of science at secondary stage.
- Practical activities to be chosen should have relevance for further life through acquisition of skills and values.
- Emphasis on the 'learner centered approach' commensurate with the physical, mental, social and emotional development of learners in relevant age groups. In other words, there needs a shift of emphasis from information based and teacher-centered education to process centered and learner friendly education. Learners are needed to be encouraged to work both individually as well as in groups.
- Critical, creative and generative thinking has to be developed.
- Improvisation should be encouraged but designing would also be provided as a component in exploration.
- Flexibility in experimentation needs to be widely promoted.
- Teachers could help the learners devise appropriate experimentation and activities within and outside the school.

The present science education is far away from the above vision. Science is being taught in the schools as a body of established facts obtained by individuals using infallible methods. The present classroom practices emphasize on the product side of science rather than the method of acquiring the knowledge, which is the scientific method that forms the process side of science. In spite of several recommendations by many associations, AAAS (American Association for the Advancement of Science), SAPA (Science A Process Approach), NSTA (National Science Teachers

Association) to develop science process skills, science related attitudes, understanding of nature of science along with acquisition of knowledge, still there is a very little chance provided to the learners to acquire the above.

In the conventional classroom, the classes are usually driven by "teacher talk" and depend heavily on textbooks for the structure of the course. Teachers serve as pipelines and seek to transfer their thoughts and meanings to the passive students. Thus, there is little room for student initiated questions and independent thought or interaction between students. Added to this, the present curricula in science and mathematics is overstuffed and undernourished (NCERT, 1968). They emphasize the learning of answers more than the exploration of questions, memory at the expense of critical thought, bits and pieces of information instead of understanding in context, recitation over argument, reading in lieu of doing. They fail to encourage students to work together, to share ideas and information freely with each other, or to use modern instruments to extend their intellectual capabilities. Above all, there is no scope of understanding the misconceptions found among the students in the conventional method of teaching science.

Apart from the above observations, it was also found (Sood, 1964) that the teachers do not concentrate on the process of learning by students and also overlook the misconceptions among them. The Chinese proverb "Do not give the fish but teach the person how to catch a fish" can be remembered here. Teaching the children how to learn is important than providing the facts to them. It is expected to raise the application abilities among the children learning science and technology to meet the aspirations of the day. Besides this, in the present competing world, there is a need of objective, critical and an intellectual mind i.e. a proper scientific attitude.

All the above ideas and processes occur repeatedly in constructivist writings. Even the students who score well are unable to successfully integrate or contrast memorized facts and formulate real-life applications outside the school-room (Yager, 1991). It was also found that practical knowledge and school knowledge are becoming mutually exclusive; many students see little connection between what they learn in the classroom and with their real life.

One proposed solution for the problem is to prepare students to become good adaptive learners. Obviously, the traditional teacher-as-information-giver, textbook guided classroom has failed to bring about the desired outcomes of science education. An alternative is to change the focus of the classroom from teacher dominated to student centered using a constructivist approach. Studies have proved that constructivist approach is effective in the development of science attitudes and achievement by using various methods and strategies.

An attempt was made to study the effectiveness of constructivist approach in indian context at secondary school level to find out whether this method would improve the students' understanding of nature of science, demonstrate a superior understanding of basic science concepts, use and understand basic processes of science better, can apply science concepts and processes in new situations, have more positive attitudes of science, science study, and science teachers, develop better science process skills including observing, reasoning, inferring, interpreting, proposing solutions, and predicting consequences, and have more complete views of the nature of science.

Statement of the Problem

Constructivism is a view of learning based on the belief that knowledge is not a thing that can be simply given by the teacher at the front of the room to students in their desks. Rather, learners through an active, mental process of development construct knowledge; learners are the builders and creators of meaning and knowledge. The teacher is a co-participant, facilitator unlike the conventional one. The student is an active participant who explores, constructs the meaning, explains it and expands the knowledge with the help of the questions posed by the teacher. Constructivist approach is a pupil-centered method of teaching.

The present investigation is titled as

"Effectiveness of constructivist approach on students' achievement in science, scientific attitude and perception of nature of science at secondary level".

Operational Definitions of the Terms Used

A number of terms and concepts have been used in the study. To convey the specific meaning, the terms and concepts used in the present study have been defined operationally as follows.

(i) Constructivist Approach

Psychological Constructivist approach is based on Jean Piaget's model of the development of the individual. The process focuses learning as a personal, individual, intellectual construction based on experiences of one in the world. Learning by doing and forming ideas from one's exploration is the underlying theory behind psychological constructivism. In this approach, the child is viewed like a scientist who possesses insights, questions, solves problems, experiments, explores and so on. During the process, the child learns many skills like observing, hypothesizing, inferring etc., which in turn develops a scientific mind and positive attitude towards science, the main objectives of teaching science.

(ii) Achievement in Science

Achievement indicates the attainment of the objectives like knowledge, understanding, application and skill. An achievement test in the selected content including all the above four levels of objectives was constructed by the investigator. Thus achievement in science in the present study is the total score obtained by the students in the achievement test constructed by the investigator.

(iii) Perception of Nature of Science

Perception of nature of science means the way the students perceive or understand the nature of science. In the present study, perception of nature of science pertains to the following aspects:

(a) Characteristics of science

(b) Scientific methods/processes

(c) Use of scientific discoveries

(d) Application of science in daily life

(e) Role of science in society and its impact on human beings.

(iv) Science Process Skills

In science, the ways of thinking, measuring, solving problems and using thoughts are called processes. Among the various basic and integrated skills, the following intellectual skills were selected for the present study.

(a) Observing;

(b) Inferring;

(c) Predicting;

(d) Hypothesizing;

(e) Interpreting; and

(f) Reasoning.

The science process skills in the present study are the total sum of the above process skills in the developed test.

(v) Scientific Attitude

Scientific attitude is "the cognitive attitude or belief about thinking and has also affective and behavioural aspects"(Guilford, 1978). Among the various scientific attitudes listed earlier, the following were selected for the present study:

(a) Curiosity;

(b) Rationality;

(c) Willingness to suspend judgment;

(d) Open-mindedness;

(e) Objectivity;

(f) Perseverance; and

(g) Free from superstitions.

The scientific attitude in the present study is the total sum of the above components in the developed test.

(vi) Attitude Towards Science

Gardner (1975a) defined attitude towards science in the following manner:

"We may regard a person's attitude to science as a learned disposition to evaluate in certain ways objects, people, actions, situations or propositions involved in learning science."

The term attitude towards science is composed of two words—'attitude' and 'science'. Attitude, according to Thurstone (1929) is the degree of positive or negative effect associated with some psychological object. Object here is 'science' as a discipline.

Hence, Attitude towards Science is the generalized attitude towards the universe of science content and being measured in terms of its favourableness estimated from the scores obtained by the subject on an attitude scale towards science.

Variables Included in the Study

(A) Independent Variables

(i) Constructivist approach aims at improving achievement in science, perception of nature of science, science process skills, scientific attitude and attitude towards science.

(ii) Gender.

(B) Dependent Variables

Effect of constructivist approach is studied on the students' achievement in science, perception of nature of science, science process skills, scientific attitude and attitude towards science.

Objectives of the Study

With an insight into the philosophical, psychological and pedagogical bases of constructivism, the research undertaken aimed to study a few research bearing questions, which may throw more light upon constructivism as an approach to learning. These are reflected in the form of objectives given below:

1. To develop science lessons based on constructivist approach in the selected units of science for eighth standard students.
2. To study the effectiveness of constructivist approach on the students' achievement in science.

3. To study the effectiveness of constructivist approach on the students' perception of nature of science.

4. To study the effectiveness of constructivist approach in developing science process skills among the students.

5. To study the effectiveness of constructivist approach in developing scientific attitude among the students.

6. To study the effectiveness of constructivist approach on the students' attitude towards science.

7. To study the interaction between 'gender' and 'group' with reference to achievement in science, perception of nature of science, scientific attitude, science process skills and attitude towards science.

8. To examine the relationship among achievement in science, perception of nature of science, science process skills, scientific attitude and attitude towards science.

Hypotheses Formulated for the Study

The following research hypotheses were formulated in pursuance of the broad objectives of the study:

H1: The constructivist approach does have a positive effect on the achievement of students in science.

H2: The constructivist approach does have a positive effect on the students' perception of nature of science.

H3: The constructivist approach does have a positive effect on the development of science process skills among students.

H4: The constructivist approach does have a positive effect on the scientific attitude of students.

H5: The constructivist approach does have a positive effect on the students' attitude towards science.

H7: There is an interaction between 'gender' and 'group' on students' achievement in science, perception of nature of science, scientific attitude, science process skills and attitude towards science.

H9: There is a positive relationship among achievement in science, perception of nature of science, science process skills, scientific attitude and attitude towards science.

In the next chapter i.e. review of related literature, researches related to the present study are reviewed.

2

Review of Related Literature

Philosophical and Psychological Insights into Constructivism

The learning of science by children and older students, no less than scientific research itself, is in its own way an investigative, constructive process. The general philosophy that supports this view has come to be called constructivism which may be taken up as practice and theory still underdevelopment.

As theory, constructivism has had two major historical sources. One source is philosophical, a general theory of knowledge that can provide background and support for more specific educational theory and practice. The other source is the experiences of reflective practitioners, teachers and those who seek to help and learn from them. A third source, growing in recent times is a professional research community, seeking to bring theory and practice more coherently together.

Constructivism is not a new concept. It has its roots in philosophy and has been applied to sociology and anthropology as well as cognitive psychology and education.

Recent trends in science teaching have seen phrases such as "students construct their own knowledge" or "students construct their own knowledge based on the existing schemata and beliefs." Yet these phrases grew out of an epistemology that has been around a long time. Aspects of constructivist theory can be found among the works of Socrates, Plato, and Aristotle (ranging from 470 to

320 B.C.) all of which speak of the formation of knowledge. However, the main philosophy of constructivism is generally credited to Jean Piaget.

According to Fosnot (1993), Constructivism is derived from the field of cognitive psychology. The constructivist paradigm is based on the work of Piaget, Vygotsky and Bruner. However, it was Piaget who attempted to answer epistemological questions by scientific means. He believed that knowledge acquisition could be explained just as an evolutionary acquisition. The process of equilibration as described by Piaget implied that knowledge acquisition is a process in which the learner actively constructs his or her knowledge, which is known as Constructivism. Bruner (1966) along with Ausubel (1968) and Piaget (1973) stated that learning is an active process and students construct new ideas or concepts based on the current knowledge. Pestalozzi came to many similar conclusions more than a century earlier. His basic pedagogical innovation was his insistence that children learn through the senses rather than words. However, Piaget became regarded as the father of constructivism and provided the foundation for modern day constructivism.

Kant (1983), the first major precursor said that scientific knowledge is actively constructed from our observational experience. For Kant, the metaphor of construction is pointedly appropriate. Kantian delineation of the investigative art is found in the writings of three American philosophers namely Pierce (1839-1914), who developed the theory of abduction, the art of moving from novel phenomenon to hypothesis that would if confirmed, explain the phenomenon.

A second psychologist and philosopher was Dewey (1933) known in educational circles mainly for his association with progressive education movements. Kuhn (1970) analysed historical shifts from the presuppositions of scientific investigation and thought.

Perhaps the first constructivist philosopher, Giambatista Vico commented in a treatise in 1970 that "one only knows something if one can explain it". Basically defined, constructivism simply means that as we experience something new, we internalize it through our past experiences or knowledge that we have previously constructed.

For constructivists, learning is not knowledge written on or transplanted into a person's mind as if the mind were a blank slate waiting to be written on or an empty gallery waiting to be filled (Locke, 1969). Constructivists use the metaphor of construction because, it aptly summarizes the epistemological view that knowledge is built by individuals. Vygotsky (1978) recommended social interaction as a fundamental aspect of the development of cognition. He believed that everything is learned on two levels. First, through interaction with others and then integrated into the individual's mental structure.

Since Ausubel et al. (1978), theorists have argued that the construction of new knowledge in science is strongly influenced by prior knowledge, that is, conceptions gained prior to the point of new learning. Learning by construction thus implies a change in prior knowledge, where change can mean replacement, addition, or modification of extant knowledge. Learning, by construction, involving change is the basis of the Posner et al. (1982) conceptual change model.

According to Papert (1991), students should give themselves time to complete a task thoroughly giving their minds a chance to absorb new knowledge and allow true learning to take place. The second and third principles of learning are discussion and connections, i.e connecting new data with an already established schema to invest self-gained knowledge (Piaget, 1980). The constructivist approach to learning is constructing a new knowledge each time. In the constructivist approach, the student creates his own knowledge. Through trial and error, peer cooperation, and hands on activities, students are able to envision and discover new possibilities of and within themselves.

Lerman (1989), following Kilpatrick (1987) suggested that the core epistemological theses of constructivism are as follows: (i) knowledge is actively constructed by the cognizing subject not passively received from the environment. (ii) coming to know is an adaptive process that organizes one's experiential world. It does not discover an independent, pre-existing world outside the mind of the knower.

Later Resnick (1987) summarized constructivism in three statements:

(i) Learners construct understanding.

(ii) They do not simply mirror what they are told or what they read...to understand something is to know relationships.

(iii) Bits of isolated information are forgotten or become inaccessible to memory. All learning depends on prior knowledge.

Besides this, Glaserfeld (1984), a radical constructivist said that the realist believes his constructs to be replica or reflection of independently existing structures, while the constructivist remains aware of the experiencer's role as originator of all structures...for the constructivist there are no structures other than those which the knower constitutes by his very own activity of coordination of experiential particles.

A study conducted by Watts and Bentley (1991), made a clear distinction between 'strong' and 'weak' constructivism. They also expressed that strong constructivism centres upon cognitive construction, constructive processes, oppositional critical realism, self-determination and collegiality.

Saunders (1992) explained that constructivism could be defined as that philosophical position, which holds that any reality is in the most immediate and concrete sense; the mental construction of those who believe they have discovered and investigated it.

Brooks and Brooks (1993) explained that the constructivist vista is far more panoramic and therefore elusive. Deep understanding not imitative behavior is the goal. They claimed that teachers should not look for what students can repeat but for what they can generate, demonstrate and exhibit. They have five guiding principles of constructivism:

(i) using the problems of relevance to the students in instruction;

(ii) learning is structured around primary concepts;

(iii) valuing students' point of view;

(iv) adapting curriculum to address students suppositions; and

(v) assessing students learning in the context of teaching.

Lynn Renz, B. (1996) carried out a study to examine how constructivist principles relate to school assessment. Eleven principles for the development of a school accreditation model from a constructivist perspective were presented.

In other words, as explained by Crowther (1997) what is supposedly found is an invention whose inventor is unaware of his or her act of invention and who considers it as something that exists independently of him; the invention then becomes the basis of his or her world view and actions.

Cobb (1999) explained that constructivist learning theory predicts that knowledge encoded from data by learners themselves will be more flexible, transferable and useful than knowledge encoded for them by experts and transmitted to them by an instructor or other delivery agent. Baylor, Samsonov and Smith (1996) in their book have emphasised on constructivist approach of learning. In the fourth chapter "A collaborative class investigation into telecommunication in education", they quoted the words of Fosnot (1996) who referred constructivism as "a theory about knowledge and learning." According to constructivist theory, knowledge is "temporary, developmental, non-objective, internally constructed, socially and culturally mediated". Fosnot presented learning as "a self-regulatory process of struggling with the conflict between existing personal models of the world and discrepant new insights". Learners construct new models which are refined through "cooperative social activity, discourse and debate". It changes the dynamics of the traditional classroom by empowering the learner as the focus and architect of the learning process, while redefining the role of the instructor is to be a guide and helper rather than a source and conduct of knowledge.

In 1991, Wheatley proposed a model of constructivist teaching using the problem centred learning approach. He stated that each student must be encouraged to build his or her own conceptual constructs that will permit the ordering of knowledge into useful problem solving schema. He even projected that the teacher's role is to provide stimulating and motivational experiences through negotiation and act as a guide in the building of personalized schema.

As may be seen from the above, the trend has changed from behaviorism to constructivism i.e. construction of knowledge on ones own, based on the preexisting knowledge. In the initial stages knowledge was considered as a commodity that can be transplanted into pupils' minds. But, gradually the idea has changed and it is felt that an individual builds knowledge during the process of learning. It may be individually on their own or by interacting with others.

Studies Related to the Characteristics of Constructivist Teaching and Learning Process

Constructivism is a view of learning based on the belief that knowledge is not a thing that can be simply given by the teacher in the front of the room to students at their desks. Rather, knowledge is constructed by learners through an active mental process of development; learners are the builders and creators of meaning and knowledge. Constructivist beliefs have recently been applied to teaching and learning in the classroom. Constructivism draws on the developmental work of Piaget (1977) and Kelly (1991).

Fosnot (1989) defines constructivism with reference to four principles: learning, in an important way, depends on what we already know; new ideas occur as we adapt and change our old ideas; learning involves inventing ideas rather than mechanically accumulating facts; meaningful learning occurs through rethinking old ideas and coming to new conclusions about new ideas which conflict with our old ideas. A productive, constructivist classroom, then, consists of learner-centered, active instruction. In such a classroom, the teacher provides students with experiences that allow them to hypothesize, predict, manipulate objects, pose questions, research, investigate, imagine, and invent.

Yager (1991) suggested the procedures for constructivist teachers namely challenging the students' previous conceptions, encouraging spirit of questioning, thoughtful discussions, autonomy and initiative among the students. The students are to be encouraged to use manipulative, interactive physical materials and explore the things surrounding them. In addition to the above features, emphasis of social qualities like promoting student leadership, collaboration, location of information and taking actions as a result of the learning process; encouraging use of alternative sources of information, predicting consequences of the events; providing adequate time for reflection and analysis; respecting and use all ideas that students generate; encouraging self analysis, collection of real evidence to support ideas and reformulation of ideas in light of new knowledge were suggested. Brooks and Brooks (1993) and Clemens (2001) also suggested the characteristics of a constructivist teacher. Apart from the suggestions given by Yager (1991), it was reported that as a result of constructivist classroom, there is cognitive and affective growth, improved tolerance, civility and understanding. Students learned to value multiple perspectives, validate their own ideas and to be respectful of others and their ideas.

Inturn, Brooks and Brooks (1993) also offered an interesting comparison of the visible differences between "traditional" classroom and "constructivist" classrooms. They compared the curriculum transaction, role of teacher in the class, value placed for the students, assessment point of view and so on. They had also expressed that the students are encouraged to develop meta-cognitive skills such as reflective thinking and problem solving techniques in the constructivist approach unlike in the traditional method of learning.

In addition to the above ideas of Brooks and Brooks (1993), Insley and Lynn (1998) conducted a qualitative study on 8th grade students and their experiences in constructivist English teachers classroom. Participant observations and informal and formal interviews were key research strategies. The findings indicated that there were five significant factors which eighth graders thought were important to learning. They were: (i) creating and building positive learning environment. (ii) acknowledging of natural learning process. (iii) connecting of previous learning to current meaning making experiences. (iv) providing ongoing opportunities for students to express their unique abilities and to display their meaningful learning and (v) using small learning groups that allow for natural social process. Offering the students perspective on learning adds a powerful dimension to the literature on constructivist teaching and learning.

Constructivist teaching and learning were the focused areas of research of Gray. In his research, an insight was provided into the process of teacher change and development and raised questions about teacher professional development that had implications for the way constructivist and transactional curricula are implemented. There were philosophical and psychological arguments to support constructivist educational practices (Perkins, 1999). Philosophically, the individual has to construct or reconstruct what things mean because the stimuli we encounter are never logically sufficient to convey the message. Psychologically, research shows that active engagement in learning may lead to better retention, understanding and active use of knowledge.

Appleton (1996) conducted a study and explored a way to analyse and describe learning derived from both constructivist theoretical and classroom practice. This study resulted in a model for science lessons, which allows identification and description of students' cognitive progress through the lessons. By using this focus on the learner, it provides pre-knowledge for teachers about students that might arrive at solutions to science problems during lessons and therefore potentially indicate about appropriate teaching strategies.

While the above studies either directly or indirectly reflect the charecterstics of constructivism, Yager (2000) summarizes the characteristic features of Constructivist approach as follows:

Constructivism emphasises learning and not teaching; encourages and accepts learner autonomy and initiative; sees learners as creatures of will and purpose; thinks of learning as a process; encourages learner inquiry; acknowledges the critical role of experience in learning; nurtures learners natural curiosity; takes the learner's mental model into account; emphasises performance and understanding when assessing learning; bases itself on the principles of the cognitive theory; makes extensive use of cognitive terminology such as predict, create and analyze; considers how the student learns; encourages learners to engage in dialogue with other students and the teacher; supports co-operative learning; involves learners in real world situations; emphasises the context in which learning takes place; considers the beliefs and attitudes of the learner; provides learners the opportunity to construct new knowledge and understanding from authentic experience.

Similarly, Yagnik and Likhia (2004) gave a clear understanding in constructivist approach. They also gave a brief account of shift from behaviourism to cognitivism and then to constructivism, the historical movements in the teaching learning process and also listed down the major points of constructivism as:

(i) prior beliefs;

(ii) conceptual change;

(iii) validity of self-constructed conceptualizations;

(iv) cognitive disequilibration; and

(v) inquiry.

The goals for science education suggested by National Science Education Standards (NSES) (NRC, 2000) is to develop students who know about and understand the natural world. They can use scientific processes and principles to make decisions and should be able to engage in discourse and debate of issues related to science and technology. Finally, there is a need to develop in students the knowledge and skills of science.Recently, Shrivastava and Shrivastava (2004) also addressed the main guiding principles of constructivism as posing problems of emerging relevance to students, structuring learning around primary concepts—the quest for essence, seeking and valuing students' point of view, adopting curriculum to address students' suppositions and assessing student learning in the context of teaching.

Stevens (2004) explained the influence of behaviourism and constructivism. The research findings suggested that there are three factors which characterize the constructivist learning situations in the classrooms. They are (i) student autonomy (ii) classroom interaction (iii) cognitive exploration leading to higher order thinking skills.

Senapathy (2004) attempted to integrate digital technology into constructivist learning environment for effective learning and expressed that constructivist revolution offers a new vision of the learner as an active sense maker and suggested new methods of instruction.

The studies reviewed above focus on characteristics of constructivist approach, constructivist teachers, suggestions for the teachers following the constructivist approach, description of classroom and constructivist classroom environment.

Studies Related to the Effectiveness of Constructivist Approach on Teacher Education and Other Subject Areas

There are a number of studies conducted on attitudes, beliefs, views and behaviour of the teachers (Elaine, 1996) in a constructivist classroom. Especially, many researches have been carried out on the issues related to planning and teaching science and the role of teacher from a constructivist perspective. Scot, P., Asoko, H., Driver, R. et.al. (1991) drew attention to the following four aspects of constructivist teaching. (i) There is no unique method or instructional route for teaching a particular topic from a constructivist perspective. (ii) Learning science involves not only coming to terms with new conceptual structures but also involves developing a new rationality for knowledge. (iii) The teaching involves establishing an argument for the science view which is likely to involve empirical findings but goes beyond these in helping students to construct the particular 'ways of seeing' adopted by the science community. (iv) Teaching informed by a constructivist perspective recognized that both the practical activities and their discussion might be interpreted by students in ways that differ from those of intended.

There was a concentrated effort by Chaille and Britain (1991); Tobin and Dawson (1992); Tolman and Hardy (1995); and Louise, S.E. (2000) in studying the role of a teacher in constructivist approach. It was pointed out that in a constructivist classroom, the teacher is no longer the transmitter of knowledge but the facilitator of learning (Tobin and Dawson, 1992). The facilitator of learning needs to keep in mind that instruction will vary depending on the learners' prior knowledge (Tobin and Dawson, 1992), current interest, and level of involvement (Chaille and Britain, 1991), acquiring, understanding, using and reflecting on knowledge (Tolman and Hardy, 1995). Louise (2000) examined the role of a teacher study group in negotiating constructivist science teaching in an elementary school. The study group created a non-threatening forum for reflection, support and sharing as each teacher learned that she is not alone in the struggles and challenges they experienced in negotiating constructivism and the new science curriculum.

In connection to the above studies, Steffe and D'Ambrosio (1995) also explained the importance of activating prior knowledge by teachers. They expressed that when teachers are familiar with students' prior knowledge they can provide learning experiences to build on these existing understandings. Prior knowledge can be activated in many ways, for example, by asking students what they know, by brainstorming, by doing semantic mapping, by predicting outcomes or by performing some skill or process. Gurney (1995), Shchlenker, Yoshida and Pery (1995) also stated that articulation of prior knowledge acquaints teachers with students' thinking, affording insights from which to plan instruction. To bring out changes in the students learning, teacher's knowledge is constantly being constructed as he or she interacts with students (Simon, 1995).

Students must activate prior knowledge in order to extend and refine this knowledge. The most effective activities for knowledge use are problem-solving activities (Steffe and Gale, 1995). This encourages students to continue to examine and build on their knowledge. When students work in groups to solve problems, it is more useful than when they work alone because, they have the opportunity to constantly voice ideas and receive feedback (Chaille and Britain, 1991). Reflection refers to understanding what one knows. This requires providing activities that ask students to look back at what they have learned (Tobin and Dawson, 1992).

Research indicated that communicating knowledge is essential for understanding (Fensham and Gunstone, 1994). There are many ways in which knowledge can be shared, for example, conferencing between teacher and student, small group activities in which students voice their interpretations, oral reports, projects, role-playing and demonstrations.

A study conducted by Glynn and Duit (1993) expressed that in order to help students learn science meaningfully, teachers should ensure that learning is constructive. The constructive learning of science is a dynamic process of building, organizing, and elaborating knowledge of the natural world. In their view, students learn science meaningfully when five conditions are present: (i) existing knowledge is activated, (ii) existing knowledge is related to educational experiences, (iii) intrinsic motivation is developed, (iv) new knowledge is constructed, and (v) new knowledge is applied, evaluated, and revised. Students vary in the nature and extent of their experiences and therefore come to science class with personal mental models that vary in the degree.

A few studies were conducted to examine the beliefs, attitude, support and usage of constructivist practices by the preservice and inservice teachers in the west (Tobin and Dawson, 1992; Beard, 1995). Joseph (2000) designed a qualitative study of the beliefs and practices of a group of effective middle school teachers with respect to constructive learning and teaching environments. The results clearly showed an evidence of correlation between the beliefs and practices found in constructivism and how effective are the middle level learning and teaching environments. Constructivists are more conscious of the role of both student and the teacher in affecting cognitive development of students.

John, S.T. (2000) in his study, measured the teaching behaviours of elementary science teachers. The results of the study indicated that the teacher who understood constructivist-based science scored significantly higher on most of the CLES (Constructivist Learning Environment Survey) scales. This study allowed one to predict that a teacher who understands constructivist-based science may practice this form of pedagogy more often than a teacher who does not. According to this research, elementary teachers may avoid constructivist-based science teaching due to a lack of understanding rather than a limited time for support from principal, staff or peers.

Youngsun (2001) also investigated the pre-service teachers' understandings of the ontology and epistemology underlying constructivist notions of learning. Of the sixteen participants in the study, five significantly changed ontological and epistemological beliefs and eleven did not. Profile changes for the five who did change also resulted in changes in their conceptions of science teaching and learning. The overall conclusion drawn from this research is that pre-service teachers can develop constructivist notions of teaching that are consistent with and founded upon philosophical principles.

Palas, Denise D. (2002) in his interpretive research project examined how teachers' beliefs and attitudes about learning related to their work as mentors to student teachers. Mentors were found to embrace a non-linear, multidirectional view of learning in which learners made choices and decisions and in which teachers valued their autonomy to structure classroom time in ways that supported beliefs about active child centred learning. Finally, a theme emerged depicting the struggle of participant mentors felt as their student teachers entered the teaching field.

Later, the research focused on usage of constructivist approach in the area of teacher education. Tobin and Dawson (1992) developed a teacher survey and a student survey to determine the frequency of usage of various instructional practices by the teachers. Overall, teachers reported significant improvements in the science and mathematics curricula. The findings of this study provided evidence that: (i) teachers feel the science and mathematics curricula are much more adequate since the implementation of the systemic reform process, (ii) teachers report using a variety of constructivist strategies in their classrooms (weekly or more often); and (iii) students also report experiencing constructivist practices in their classrooms. Overall, teachers and students report using several constructivist practices in their classrooms. Moussiaux and Norman (1996) also supported the above findings.

Wing-Mui SO (2002) conducted a study that aimed to find to what extent constructivist teaching was utilized in primary science lessons. The evaluation approach used during the lesson observation pertained to a constructivist view of teaching and learning. A more detailed analysis of student teachers' performance in the six areas (of features of constructivist teaching) showed that the overall performance of student teachers in the six areas of features of constructivist teaching was moderate. Student teachers during their microteaching paid some consideration to learners' prior understanding in their teaching. Comparatively, student teachers were able to: use pupils' existing knowledge to guide teaching and devise incisive questions; provide opportunities for pupils to utilize ideas and guide pupils to generate explanations; and, alternative in a micro-teaching setting. They made frequent use of questioning to guide learners to understand new ideas. However, student teachers seemed quite satisfied with the short answers provided by learners and they seldom required learners to further elaborate on their responses.

Beard (1995) conducted a study to determine the extent of support for the new paradigm among secondary science teachers. The results of this study indicated a moderate support for the constructivist paradigm. It was found that constructivist assessment principles received less support than the teaching and learning of constructivist principles. Results of multiple regression analysis revealed gender and type of science class as having significant relationship with science teachers' perceptions of the constructivist principles. Females were significantly more supportive of the constructivist principles than the males.

In nineties the focus of constructivist approach had broadened. Number of studies were conducted to see the impact of constructivist approach on teacher education.

Terrance (2003) conducted a study to find out the effects of traditional and constructivist teaching methodologies on comprehension of content of acids and bases chemistry unit in 7th grade. A content-based assessment with a conceptual understanding component was administered at the end of the instruction and also after three weeks to test long-term memory retention. The findings seemed to indicate improved comprehension among students and improved pre-service teachers' attitudes toward teaching and learning mathematics and science. The findings of the study also speak of the need for a constructivist approach when longer-term retention is the goal.

It was also reported that constructivist teaching methods improved pre service teachers' perceptions (Moussiaux and Norman, 2000; Steffe and Gale, 1995); attitudes toward mathematics and it also helped them learn mathematics (Appleton and Asoko, 1996; Gibson, 2000) and in reducing anxiety level (Couch-Kuchey, 2002). A case study done by Appleton and Asoko (1996) to examine the impact of an in-service programme about constructivist approach on teachers' progress, found that teachers who used constructivist approach had improved in their teaching attitudes and attitude towards science. Gibson (2000) reported similar results about the impact of constructivist instructional methods on pre-service teachers' attitudes toward teaching and learning science. He also expressed that this method of teaching had a positive impact on pre service teachers' attitude towards mathematics (Gibson, Brewer, Magnier, McDonald and Van Strat, 1999). In addition, the data indicated that these instructional methods also helped preservice teachers learn mathematics.

A case study conducted by Sook (2001) also indicated that there was a positive impact on preservice teachers' understanding of physical science concepts, attitude towards science teaching and learning. It was reported that there was improvement in critical thinking skills among middle school teachers. On the contrary, principles of biology taught using a traditional approach (lecture and note taking) had a negative impact on preservice teachers interest in teaching science (Gibson and Van Strat, 2000).

Apart from the improvement in the perceptions and attitudes, it was reported that the teachers were able to prepare various assessment prototypes to prototype higher level thinking among students as a result of constructivist approach (Daigle, Marie, A. 2000). Participants in the study indicated improvement in their ability to apply constructivist principles to their standard-based classrooms.

In Indian context, Donga (2004) had investigated the theoretical and practical constructivist view of 187 secondary school teachers. The analysis of the data revealed that: (i) There was no sex difference in theoretical constructivist view of teacher as well as practice of constructivism by school teachers. (ii) There was no significant effect of teaching experience, educational qualification and professional qualities of teachers on their theoretical constructivist as well as on their use of constructivism in the practice of teaching. (iii) Most of the teachers were found to be believing in constructivism theoretically and were practising them in classroom.

Certain studies were conducted to examine the relationship between teachers' personal beliefs about how students learn mathematics and their instructional practices with regard to the mathematical achievement of secondary level students in United States (Jane, 2000). The findings suggest different dimensions of teachers' beliefs and instructional practices have differing effects on student achievement.

Yuen (2001) conducted a study to develop the constructivist behaviours among four new science teachers prepared at University of Iowa. The results indicated that the new teachers were largely early constructivist teachers. The new teachers shared arrange of constructivist behaviours that correspond to national standards including: (i) students sharing the responsibility of learning with teachers; (ii) student engagement in activities and experiences; (iii) students with positive attitudes who are motivated to learn; (iv) teaching that focuses on student relevance; (v) variation in teaching approaches and assessments; (vi) establishing a friendly, non judgmental learning environment; (vii) teaching that incorporates higher order thinking skills and the use of scientific knowledge and ideas; (viii) teacher understanding of subject matter and integration of content and science process skills in context; (ix) teacher as intellectual, reflective practitioner.

Heeyoung (2001) conducted a study to determine whether the present Korean teacher education programme for secondary school teachers was effective in improving teacher understanding of constructivism and STS, because the current Korean National Science Curriculum emphasized both ideas as reforms. After the treatments in the pre-service and in-service teacher education programmes, the teachers were inclined to agree with ideas of constructivism and STS. Pre-service programme was more effective than that of in service programmes in improving teachers' perspectives of both constructivist and science technology and society (STS).

Watts and Fofili (1998) explained the notion of 'constructivist teaching' and discussed as it featured within the debates on constructivist research in science classrooms. An argument was then made that constructivist teaching itself should be superceded in favour of 'critical constructivism', an approach which undertakes a broader critique of the relationships between teacher and the taught, between learner and subject matter and between schooling and society. Some data was also presented in this article from a study of Brazilian teachers moving from constructivism towards critical constructivism through an in-service professional development course and a series of action research projects.

James, D.M. (2000) explored the learning-to-teach process of four first-year high school teachers, all graduates of a constructivist-based science education program known as Teacher Education Environments in Mathematics and Science (TEEMS). The pedagogical perspectives apparent among the participants in this study emerged as six patterns in teaching method: (i) utilization of grouping strategies; (ii) utilization of techniques that allow the students to help teach; (iii) similar format of daily instructional strategy; (iv) utilization of techniques intended to promote engagement; (v) utilization of review strategies; (vi) assessment by daily monitoring and traditional tests and vii. restructuring content knowledge.

Michael, J. (2001) examined the theoretical discourse over constructivism in education and empirically studied the shift in one teacher's praxis as he moves from individual constructivist pedagogy to social constructivist pedagogy. Two significant dilemmas appeared through study of discourse and practice of social and individual forms of constructivism. First, taking constant stance towards teaching can create an illusion for a teacher committed to discipline based pedagogy. Secondly, the empirical study raised questions about the enterprise of reading in constructivist classrooms.

Geelan (1995) in his study expressed that number of different, flexible strategies must be combined if curriculum development is to be truly constructivist in its perspective; there is no single 'right way'. Matrix technique is offered as one possible way of organizing the ideas, knowledge, discussion and inquiry of students in science classrooms, with the intention of promoting the individual and social construction of viable knowledge. Its particular contribution is seen to be in the area of facilitating the critical synthesis of ideas of students from a variety of disciplines in seeking solutions to relevant, motivating problems from the human world. The introduction of constructivist reforms should ideally occur through meaningful negotiation of both: (i) the learning environment; and (ii) ideas about knowing and learning with students.

Harcombe (2001) breaks new ground demonstrating that when professional teacher development is based on constructivist learning theory and framed in the knowledge domain of the sciences, it empowers teachers to dramatically change what they know, how they teach, and what their students learn.

Saunders (1992) proposed a four-step constructivist approach to teaching science; Hands-on investigative labs that are problem centred and where there are no prescribed methods or procedures to solve the problem or exploring the phenomena. Firstly, in using this inquiry approach, students formulate expectations about what is likely to be observed. Secondly, there is an active cognitive involvement—learning is made meaningful through activities like thinking aloud, developing alternative explanations, interpreting data, participating in cognitive conflict and development of alternative hypothesis. Thirdly, students work in small groups—this stimulates a higher level of cognitive activity among larger number of students than listening to lectures and also there are expanded opportunities for cognitive restructuring. Lastly, there is scope for higher level assessment of hands-on investigation, cognitive involvement and group collaboration.

Lyons, Carol A. (1996) reported the activities in which the teacher leaders engaged during session on the constructivist approach during the 1996 Teacher Leader Institute. The authors outlined five principles of learning that provided a framework for the session and discussed how participants constructed an understanding of leadership. The characteristics of positive demonstration lessons identified by participating teacher leaders were given. Finally, constructing a plan of action was discussed and a 10-point plan of action developed by small groups of teacher leaders was presented.

Zeigler (2000) examined the relationships between the perceptions of constructivist practices contained in the National Education Longitudinal Study of 1988. The findings suggested that different dimensions of constructivist teaching, learning and supervisory practices have differing effects on student achievement. The results confirm research supporting positive effect of constructivist learning practices. Specifically, an emphasis on problem solving was positively related to student achievement in mathematics. The results of the study also suggested that school setting, mathematics certification, teaching experience, gender and minority status are all factors related to the use of constructivist teaching, learning and supervisory practices.

Sanf-Chong (1997) conducted a study on teacher understanding of the nature of science and its impact on student learning about the nature of science in STS/constructivist classrooms. The results indicated that students who were taught by STS/constructivist teachers with high TOUS scores moved toward "congruent" views concerning the nature of science on a number of VOSTS items. Also, students who were taught by more traditional teachers with low TOUS scores moved toward "naive" views. The findings supported the fact that teachers who know more about the nature of science and who practice many of the STS/Constructivist teaching strategies assist students in learning more about the nature of science.

Freedman (1998) conducted a study on constructivist assessment practices. Varieties of assessment practices, wherein students were given multiple opportunities to show their competence were included. Alridge, Fraser and Taylor (2000) undertook a study to validate and use constructivist learning environment scale (CLES) in Chinese and English version.

Scricco, et al. (2000) conducted a study to help the foreign language teachers understand the importance of constructivist theory in education and how this pedagogy has helped to make computer integration possible in all disciplines.

Gold (2001) conducted a study on the impact of constructivist approach to online training for on line teachers, examined the pedagogical role of the teacher in on line education. This study investigated a two-week faculty development pedagogical training course aimed at preparing teachers to operate effectively within the online environment. The findings of the study are: (i) Online distance learning courses encourage more student participation than traditional face-to-face course. (ii) In online distance learning courses teachers and students can produce learning outcomes better than traditional face-to-face course. (iii) Online distance learning courses have more student-to-student interaction than their counter parts. This result validated the other studies on faculty views towards extrinsic versus intrinsic rewards.

Allen (2001) using an eight month, quasi-fieldwork approach and depth interviews examined how the staff of pioneer station high school constructed personal meaning for a decade long district initiative to restructure their school using outcomes-based education. The study recommended that administrators rethink the traditional, single-reality, cause-effect world view and consider a constructivist worldview that supports the existence of multiple realities, multiple paths to understanding, and the possibility of influencing rather than directing change. It outlined a framework for constructing a better understanding of the change process, and it cautions administrators to respect the power of the culture of their schools.

Constructivist approach was tried out in various areas apart from teacher education. It was noticed that many studies were conducted to find the effectiveness of constructivist approach on mathematics and language learning (Pena-Perez, Beatriz, 2000). One among them was the study conducted by Kim (1994), found that students in constructivist-mnemonic classes appeared to have a better understanding than the other students. Females retained significantly than their counterparts.

Research in the area of mathematics education revealed that constructivist-based instructional programme improved achievement and problem solving ability among the students (Smith, 1997). In contrast to the above findings, Volney (2002) in his study found that behaviourist group significantly outperformed the constructivist group on both subscales on both the immediate and delayed posttests. But the attitude scales revealed no significant differences in pretest posttest scores (Gray, 1994; Grigoruk, Melissa Sue Wright (1997). Added to these findings Reynolds, Theodara, H. (1995) had undertaken a project to address gender issues in mathematics classroom. The results showed a significant difference in the gender and cognitive issues in the mathematics classroom.

Apart from the above findings, constructivist approach also has significant impact in promoting change in students across all classes and groups (Kretschmer, 1995; Herman,1995). Added to this, it was also revealed that constructivism advocated play as the centre of early child hood curriculum (Levin, 1996).

Janice (2000) conducted a case study focused on the voice of the child as he/she developmentally and cognitively constructed meaning from the beginning of written pieces to the end. It was assumed that the sense of constructivism in the prior knowledge and meanings were created by the learner in response to encounters with ideas, people or things and art brought by the student of the learning situation. Some of the findings were: (i) Children build on positive and negative experiences in their lives and use portions of these at various times in their written work. (ii) Children require time to express thoughts to other adults or peers because it helps them to put their framework of ideas into a writing perspective. (iii) Children imitate writing that is modelled for them. (iv) Some who do not have teaching experience in their life rely on imagination. (v) Teachers' attitude affect the final product of the child.

It was found that the principles of constructivist approach were also successful in music teacher's class (Chi-Der, 2000) and also in a national movement towards "Open education" (Minho, 2001).

In Indian context, constructivist ideas are not new. There are many age old beliefs held about ancient education system prevailed in India, that it is very dogmatic, teacher centered etc. But some of the Vedic literature like Upanishads show that students in ancient days constructed knowledge on their own using their sense data, reflective experiences, inductive and deductive analysis, auguments, discussions, intellectual discourses, exploration, experimentation etc. Just as one may see in Chandogyopanishad, the formal instruction by the teacher begins only after he has been tested for what knowledge he has constructed on his own through a project that he has been assigned with (Manjula Rao, 2006). Thus we may see in several Upanishads, where learning is constructed through various methods by the students. Concept of constructivism is introduced as a part of teacher education programme in Kerala, where in the teacher trainees are trained to prepare lesson plans based on constructivist approach and take up classes during practice-in-teaching time. Banasthali Womens' Deemed University, Rajasthan is also following constructivist approach in training preservice teachers under the name 'Anveshana' which means innovation. This was tried out for a period of two years on trial basis and found successful on students' learning.

The studies reviewed above in this section attempted to examine the attitudes, beliefs, views, behaviour and use of constructivist approach in the classroom by both preservice and inservice teachers. Some of the studies have also explored the difference between constructivist classroom and a conventional classroom and also the role of teacher in a constructivist classroom. Few researches also evidenced the improvement of preservice and inservice teachers perceptions, attitudes towards mathematics and science and reduction of their anxiety level as an effect of constructivist teaching methods. It was also found that the constructivist principles were effective in bringing out improvement in the students learning among pre-service teachers in India.

Studies Related to the Effectiveness of Constructivist Approach in Science Education

An old adage states, "I hear and I forget, I see and I remember, I do and I understand" (Woolnough, 1994; p. 25), which seems to sum up, from a pupil's perspective, difficulties that might be associated with science learning.

Teaching science through investigation improves the students' achievement, their attitudes towards science; mastery of science process skills; problem solving; and creativity (Shymansky, Kyle, and Alport, 1982). While "hands-on" activities can evolve into closed-ended recipes (Walberg, 1984), true open-ended inquiry can more closely approach the notion of "minds-on". Cobern (1996) argued that science education research and curriculum development efforts in non-western countries could benefit by adopting a constructivist view of science and science learning. The goals for science education suggested by National Science Education Standards (NSES) (NRC, 2000) is to develop students who know about and understand the natural world. They can use scientific processes and principles to make decisions and should be able to engage in discourse and debate of issues related to science and technology. Finally, there is a need to develop in students the knowledge and skills of science. Constructivism offers a very different view of science and science learning assuming that the logical thinking is an inherently human quality regardless of culture and instead focuses attention on the processes of interpretation that lead to understanding. Constructivism leads on to expect that students from different cultures will have somewhat different perspectives on science.

Sahlstrom and Lindblad (1998) addressed two questions: how is student work constructed in the science classroom and how are students' science lessons related to the construction of their school careers. Using a lesson on magnetic fields as a case analysis, the study reported large differences between the lessons of the two focused students in terms of opportunities for learning both about science and about their social identities. The differences found between the two girls in terms of the development of their grades and their social networks in the class seemed to be closely mirrored in the classroom interaction.

Regina (1996) also conducted a study sought to determine the effects of prior knowledge and instructional patterns on academic achievement of 9th grade students (Ausubel, 1960; Tharp and Gallimores, 1988; Flick, Dickinson and Lederman, 2000). The findings of the study were: (i) There was a significant difference in academic achievement found between students with low and high prior knowledge; (ii) There was a significant difference in meta-cognition between students with low and high prior knowledge levels; (iii)There was no significant interaction between prior knowledge levels and instructional patterns on the academic achievement of students in global studies.

Related to the above findings, it was also found that during the process of construction of knowledge, there is a change in schema structure. It is explored in the study conducted by Ismael (1999). He investigated the schema structure of students for human evolution, their idiosyncratic conceptual change after visiting a museum exhibition, the role of alternative frameworks during learning, and the function of affect in learning. The research findings provided evidence for museum exhibition developers to embrace a schema-constructivist theory of knowledge and learning in the creation of exhibitions, which actively engage the learner in conceptual change.

Added to the above findings, Baker and Piburn (1997) investigated the process of constructing science in middle and secondary school classrooms. It was reviewed by Harris (1999) who discussed about how to bring about constructivist learning in a classroom. It was said that constructivist education requires that the learners' prior knowledge be taken into account from the out set—telling them what is correct, just doesn't work. Instead, show them generate those insights in the minds of our students. Textbooks reduce science to its least common denominator on lecture format teaching. Any dialogue that takes place within a single voice is no dialogue at all and is inconsistent with the constructivist perspective.

Research was carried out to compare the student's epistemological beliefs of constructivist versus objectivist learning situations by Windschitl and Andre (1998). The constructivist approach resulted in significantly greater conceptual change than the objectivist approach for 2 of 6 commonly held alternative conceptions; the other 4 of 6 areas showed no significant differences for treatment group. The treatment interacted significantly with epistemological beliefs. Individuals with more advanced epistemological beliefs learned more with a constructivist treatment; individuals with less developmentally advanced beliefs learned more with an objectivist treatment.

Related findings occur in research conducted by Ibrahim (2001) examined the impact of the guided constructivist teaching method on students' misconceptions about concepts of Newtonian physics. The results of the study indicate that: (i) Guided constructivist group had significantly higher mean than the other group. (ii) Significant relationship was found between achievement, conceptual structures and beliefs about content. (iii) No statistically significant difference was found between the two methods on achievement of males and females. (iv) Greater conceptual learning was fostered when teachers use interactivity based teaching strategies.

Besides this, Richmond and Striley (1996) conducted a study to understand the process by which students solve scientific problems, the difficulties students encounter in developing the requisite pieces of scientific arguments while negotiating their social roles and the ways these roles shape task engagement and the development and articulation of the arguments themselves. The results demonstrated not only that knowledge building involves the construction of scientifically appropriate arguments but that the extent to which this knowledge building takes place depends on students learning to use tools of the scientific community; their expectations about the intellectual nature of the tasks and their role in carrying these tasks out; and the access they have to the appropriate social context in which to practice developing skills.

Hand, Treagust and Vance (1994) investigated the issues related to curriculum implementation, pedagogical skills and the processes of social construction of knowledge extensively for a period of 4 years. They examined students' perceptions of the changing nature of the secondary science classrooms as a consequence of the implementation of constructivist approaches. The results of the study indicated that the students were not only appreciative of the opportunity to use their own ideas and knowledge but were also aware of the changing roles and responsibilities required of them within the classroom. It was also indicated a clearer understanding of group interactions needed to be developed in terms of developing social construction of knowledge as a more powerful learning approach.

In most of the following studies, a control group students were exposed to traditional methods of science instruction, while the experimental group students were exposed to constructivist methods of science instruction (Terrance, 2001; Brass and Jobling, 1992; Ann, 2000; Janet Hatley, 1999; Chun-Yen and Song-Ling, 1998; Banet, 1997, Ertepinar and Geban, 1996; Kim, 1994; Carey, Susan and Smith, Carol, 1993; Geban, Askar and Ozkan, 1992; Gibson, 1998; Jaus, 1977; Mattheis and Nakayama, 1988; Padilla, Okey and Garrand, 1984; Purser and Renner, 1983; Saunders and Shepardson, 1987; Scheider and Renner, 1980; Selim and Shrigley, 1983; Shrigley, 1990; Wheatley, 1990; Wollman and Lawson, 1978). In all these studies, it was concluded that inquiry-based science activities have positive effects on students' science achievement (Kim, 1994; Banet, 1997) and attitudes toward science and school, cognitive development, laboratory skills, science process skills and understanding of science knowledge as a whole when compared to students taught using a traditional approach.

Added to the above studies, Jeanne (1999) in the study explored that constructivist approach was also effective in developing students sense of self, social aspects and academic aspects. Later, Caprio (2000) also offered many personal insights on his perception of student learning. The students in the constructivist group seemed more confident of their learning and he gave them more material for independent learning. It was also found that the students in the constructivist class seemed to like class better, had more energy and took more responsibility for their learning.

Similar findings were obtained by Foxx et al. (2001). They examined the influence of constructivist pedagogy on critical thinking skills, science fair participation and level of performance. It was found that participation in science fairs and constructing a science project helped students to develop the attitudes, skills and knowledge that helped them to be comfortable and discovering the nature of science. Blunck and Yager (1990) also, in their investigation found that students in classes taught with a constructivist approach are able to develop more science creativity skills, positive attitudes toward science, understanding of the nature of science and accurate perceptions concerning science careers when compared to students in classes taught with a textbook-oriented approach.

The study conducted by Hatley (1999) also reported change in the cognitive development as a result of constructivist approach. In contrast to the findings of the studies reported above, in this study neither group showed significant changes in attitudes toward science over the course of the semester. Both groups demonstrated gains in content knowledge; the gain in the experiment group was significantly greater than the gain in the control group (Hanley, 1994). At risk students in the experimental group exhibited significant gains in content achievement and logical thinking. Similar to the above findings, the study conducted by Terrance (2001) found out the effects of traditional and constructivist teaching methodologies on comprehension of content of acids and bases chemistry unit in 7th grade. It was found that constructivist approach was effective in improving comprehension and longer-term retention.

In contrast to the above findings, Sherri (1995) in his study examined the effects of a constructivist-learning environment on student cognition of mechanics and attitude towards science compared to students enrolled in a traditional lecture course. He found that even though there were no significant differences in the two groups, qualitatively students said they enjoyed the constructivist strategies; instructor interaction, hands-on-activities and applications to everyday life.

Anyanechi, Carolyn, M.E. (1996) also investigated the use of a constructivist model to teach science to senior secondary school students in Nigeria. The treatment group was encouraged to work in groups using the local materials and in all other deliberations. The use of a constructivist model created a better and broader experiencing environment and understanding. The findings of the study not only proved the effectiveness of constructivist model but also suggested different approaches to science teaching. It was also revealed that the familiar instructional materials might have had contributed to enhancing students' cognitive styles.

Fouad (2000) explored the effects of constructivist approach using computer projected simulations and interactive engagement methods on senior secondary level i.e. 12th grade students. The results showed that there was marked improvement in understanding of Newtonian mechanics and on attitudes towards physics. It was also revealed from the result of the study conducted by Thomas (1996) that constructivist-learning environments had positive impact on motivation along with achievement.

Adams (1997) investigated the relationships between student beliefs about the nature of science, student attitudes and conceptual change about the nature of forces with in a traditional and within constructivist high school physics classroom. In the constructivist classroom (i) students saw physics as relevant and useful; (ii) there was no difference in worldview or agreement with the teachers' views on the nature of science between high and low conceptual change students; (iii) students appreciated the importance of empirical evidence and (iv) low conceptual change students had low classroom engagement. In this study it was found that the students taught by constructivist model have perceived science as relevant and useful to every day experience and also appreciated the importance of empirical evidence. Banet and Nunez (1997) made use of constructivist approach in teaching and learning about human nutrition for students of secondary level. The results showed how most of the students participated in this programme reorganized their ideas concerning the nutritional process and achieved a fuller understanding of process of nutrition in humans. The students taught by conventional method based on the teacher explanation and textbooks tended to have erroneous or incomplete ideas concerning the nutritional process.

Pooran (2000) examined the use of approaches to teaching science based on two contrasting perspectives in learning, social constructivist and traditional and their effects on students' attitudes and achievement. With constructivist-based teaching, students showed more favourable attitude towards science as a subject (Blunck, S.M., and Yager, R.E. 1990; Larry, D. Yore, 1997 and Latchman, 2000), obtained higher scores in class achievement, total achievement and achievement on the knowledge and application test. Students in the traditional group showed more favourable attitude towards school. Females showed more positive attitude towards the importance of science and obtained significantly higher scores in class achievement. No significant interaction effects were obtained for method of instruction by gender.

Preece and Baxter (2000) had done a survey of the superstitious and pseudo-scientific beliefs of 2159 secondary school students. Gender differences were found at all ages with females generally less sceptical than males. Many school students were very gullible.

Research evidenced that the constructivist approach was effective in fostering science process skills like observation, encouraging hypotheses and their testing and comparing (Hyang-Lim, 1995). Added to this Brass and Duke (1995) also found that constructivist approach is effective in developing the science skills namely formulate a hypothesis, design an experiment to test the hypothesis, note changes which occur and to record their findings in some way, observe using the senses, measuring, estimating, classifying, interpreting the results and to draw conclusions and use of variety of research techniques in their investigations.

Supplementing the above findings, Hyang-Lim (1995) conducted a study with younger children to understand changes in a target child's reasoning about water dynamics, specifically draining and movement of water in tubes. The study is important in providing an analysis that demonstrates that children in water activities are not "just playing" but that when materials and interventions challenge children's reasoning; they do in fact make progress in knowledge and reasoning. Teacher interventions that promoted progress in reasoning included fostering observation of regularities, encouraging hypotheses and their testing, fostering comparisons and promoting consciousness of actions and reactions.

A quasi-experimental study conducted by Henry (1995) to see whether a constructivist-based approach to science instruction could help fifth grade students improve scientific literacy, revealed that students in classroom that used a constructivist-based approach to science instruction were able to frame research questions, recognize blind alleys, and use science ideas, processes and inquiry. With regard to creativity, students in the classrooms that used a constructivist-based approach to science instruction demonstrated autonomy, took advantage of serendipitous situations, used local resources and displayed diversity of projects. Students showed independence in conducting projects and positive feelings about science in class and outside of class.

Marie (2002) investigated and revealed that the study provides a strong support for a positive relationship between constructivist learning environment and student attitudes, but little support for a direct relationship to student achievement in Algebra and Biology. Multiple regression findings showed that neither overall constructivist-learning environment nor standards-based teaching practices predicted achievement in any of the content areas. Overall, constructivist learning environment and standards-based teaching practices were significant positive predictors of student intrinsic value and learning strategies in all three content areas, after controlling for student and classroom demographic variables. Overall, both the practices were also significant positive predictors of self-efficacy in Algebra.

Yore and Shymansky (2000) focused verification of the use of students' perceptions and attitudes and teachers' self-report information as measures of interactive-constructivist science teaching in elementary schools. The students' perceptions of their teacher's teaching were slightly positive to positive (2.08-2.67), while students' attitudes toward science learning were somewhat more positive (2.19-2.63). Teachers' self-reported use of students' ideas, applications of science to the children's world, and use of print resources were positive (3.63-4.07). Significant ($p = 0.05$) main effects in the ANOVAs were found for students' view of constructivist approach, students' perception of use of literature in science, students' attitude toward school science, students' attitude toward the nature of science, students' attitude toward careers in science, and teachers' report of using print resources.

Speering and Rennie (1996) found in their investigation that as students move through school, attitudes to school in general, and science in particular, become less positive. This paper reports on a longitudinal study, which mapped, from the students' point of view, the transition between primary and secondary school in Western Australia. The study focused on the subject of science, and used both quantitative and qualitative methods. During the transition, there is a considerable change in the organisation of the school, the curriculum and the teacher-student relationship. Students in this study, especially the girls, were generally disenchanted with the teaching strategies used in their secondary science classrooms, and regretted the loss of the close teacher-student relationship of their primary school years. Their perceptions were that, science in secondary school was not what they had expected, and this experience may have long term implications for their subject and career choices.

In the similar lines Lucas and Roth (1996) conducted a study which was designed to investigate the relationship between students' views of the nature of scientific knowledge and their own learning of physics, and the evolution of this relationship over time. Twenty-three students were enrolled in a physics course that emphasised laboratory work and discussions about the nature of science. Changes in students' views concerning the nature of scientific knowledge and of the science teaching and learning process, which were not always complementary, are described with the aid of a model. The findings of this research have direct relevance to the planning and implementation of science courses in which the development of understandings of the nature of science is an objective.

Salim (1997) investigated the effect of guided constructivism and expository instructional methods on the attitudes of students towards physics. The results showed that the experimental group had significantly higher means than the control groups on all criterion variables. A significant interaction was found between groups and performance levels in the following cases: (a) criterion variable of attitude toward physics; (b) views toward physics learning; and (c) enjoyment of physics. This result indicated that the low performing students among the experiment group had greater gain in attitude toward physics than the high performing students in the same group. On the other hand, there was no interaction occurred between treatment groups and gender which shows that, in this study gender has no significance on attitude towards physics. Significant interaction between treatment groups and cognitive levels were found on the criterion variables of beliefs about physics as a process of learning and enjoyment of physics.

Tsai (1999) conducted a study, which viewed STS instruction as a promising means to help students' progress towards constructivist oriented epistemological views of science. It was an experimental study, wherein 101 Taiwanese female 10th graders were involved and the treatment was given for a period of eight months. The results of the study indicate that STS group students at the final stage of the study tended to have scientific epistemological views more oriented to constructivist views of science than traditional group subjects. Students' in-depth interviews revealed that some STS group students as a result of STS instruction tended to accept the theory—laden quality of scientific exploration and perceive the importance of social negotiations in science community and cultural impacts on science.

A survey done by Lamar (2001) to examine 152 students' perceptions of constructivist pedagogy indicated no significant difference in the perceptions of male and female, or higher and lower achieving students regarding constructivist pedagogy. There was significant difference in the perceptions of visual and tactile learners regarding constructivist instruction.

It is revealed from the above studies that investigative methods and inquiry-based science activities have positive effects on students' science achievement, attitude towards science and school. Many studies explored the effectiveness of constructivist approach on the improvement of laboratory skills, science process skills, understanding of scientific knowledge, development of sense of self, social and academic aspects and critical thinking among the students. Number of correlation studies have been conducted to see the relation between constructivist learning environment and achievement and attitude towards science.

In India, National Curricular Framework, (2005) highlighted the importance of constructivist approach emphasizing learning as a process of the construction of knowledge and learners actively construct their own knowledge by connecting new ideas to existing ideas on the basis of materials/activities presented to them. In this connection, NCERT has taken up a long-term project wherein the textbooks and teachers handbooks will be developed based on constructivist principles at school level to improve the quality of education.

The above studies discussed about the positive effects of constructivism although there have been some critical observations on constructivism (Suchting, 1992; Matthews, 1993; Phillips, 1995; Osborne, 1996), and some urging caution in its adoption (Millar, 1989; Solomon, 1993), few would dispute Fensham's claim that 'The most conspicuous psychological influence on curriculum thinking in science since 1980 has been the constructivist view of learning' (Fensham, 1992).

Mathews (1998) quoting New Zealand which has embraced constructivist learning approach to science curriculum, expresses that the role of the teacher as being helping students learn how to learn; being a learner too; ensuring equity for all students; creating a friendly, supportive learning enviornment; providing learning opportunities; listening to students; using the students' ideas, experiences, and interests; challenging sensitively the ideas of students; providing resources to help students learn; ensuring students communicate in a variey of modes; identify and nurturing the scientific talent and interests of all students. This list has everything except knowing the subject matter to be taught, and being able to teach it in a clear, engaging, and understandable manner." And also criticised that some concepts don't lend themselves well to a constructivist approach (molecules, potential energy, atoms, etc.).

Good and his colleagues believed that though the term construction is attractive to educators, the idea of "knowledge construction" may actually be misleading (Good, Wandersee and St. Julien, 1993). They urge educators to exercise caution before going down this road, because our view of how the mind works is continually being revised, the best strategy may be to reserve judgment about constructivism while monitoring how it compares with new theories of learning and the findings of cognitive science. Good and his colleagues state that "learning may be more than just 'carpentry' and teaching may be more than just 'negotiation' and 'building inspection".

In turn Michael R. Matthews (2000) also expressed that Constructivism is undoubtedly a major theoretical influence in contemporary science and mathematics education. Although constructivism began as a theory of learning, it has progressively expanded its dominion, becoming a theory of teaching, a theory of education, a theory of the origin of ideas, and a theory of both personal knowledge and scientific knowledge. Indeed constructivism has become education's version of the 'grand unified theory'."

Constructivism has done a service to science and mathematics education: by alerting teachers to the function of prior learning and extant concepts in the process of learning new material, by stressing the importance of understanding as a goal of science instruction, by fostering pupil engagement in lessons, and other such progressive matters. But, liberal educationalists can rightly say that these are pedagogical common places, the recognition of which goes back at least to Socrates. It is clear that the best of constructivist pedagogy can be had without constructivist epistemology – Socrates, Montaigne, Locke, Mill, and Russell are just some who have conjoined engaging, constructivist-like, pedagogy with non-constructivist epistemology.

Constructivism has also done a service by making educators aware of the human dimension of science: its fallibility, its connection to culture and interests, the place of convention in scientific theory, the historicity of concepts, the complex procedures of theory appraisal, and much else. But again realist philosophers can rightly maintain that constructivism does not have a monopoly on these insights. They can be found in the work of thinkers as diverse as Mach, Duhem, Bachelard, Popper, and Polanyi. Michael Mathews (2000) concluded that given the influence of constructivism on education reform, teacher education, curriculum development and pedagogy, it is important to be clear about just what are, and are not, the epistemological commitments of constructivism, and what relationship these commitments have, if any, to classroom practice. The history of education is littered with 'ideas that seemed good at the time', but whose enactment caused educational and cultural havoc. Constructivism has all the earmarks of being such an idea.

In spite of the above arguments and criticisms which are not totally in favour of Constructivism, there are several countries which have based their school curriculum, classroom instruction and material preparation on constructivist principles. Though one of the criticism (Michael, R. Matthews, 2000) which labels Constructivism as the "Oldwine in new bottles"; attention may be drawn to the hard realities of the classroom where science is not learnt by doing; but through monotonous teaching that is neither inspiring nor creates any voluntary thinking among children. The aim of science teaching as observed in general seemed to be more towards providing information and examination oriented. More emphasis is given to the quantitative aspect 'how much one has learnt' rather than 'how well one has learnt' which speaks of the quality of learning. As seen through various experimental studies, there is already a paradigm shift in science education "Learning how to learn" and viewing the environment from child's point of view have become the main core dimension of science teaching. Various methods and activities were evolved as a process of constructing knowledge in the classrooms. The students were actively engaged in discovery, inquiry, experiments, field observations, sharing experiences, discussions, reflections and so on. There is a need to bring desirable changes in science teaching by making it more a performing, creative and an interactive process through constructivist approach, which would bring a meaning to learning.

Insights from Review

Even though the constructivist philosophy is very old, research on its effectiveness in the field of education in particular is of recent origin. It is hopeful sign that research on constructivist approach is generally receiving due importance.

The overview of the researches related to historical development of constructivist approach and its effectiveness on teacher education, science education crystallized some of the issues and observations that may help in framing hypotheses, adopting quasi-experimental design and employing statistical techniques for analysis of data for the present study.

The studies carried out in sections II and III were experimental, correlational, comparative and descriptive in nature. Preservice and inservice teachers were the focus of the studies. Certain studies conducted are of survey type on the beliefs, values, attitudes, behaviour and the role of teachers in a constructivist classroom. Constructivist principles were tried out on pre-service teachers and found that they have improved in their epistemological beliefs, attitude, understanding of nature of science and so on.

The result of review of related literature made clear that there is lot of research conducted on historical development of constructivism than on its practice. In considering about the effectiveness of constructivist approach on students, the studies reviewed in the west concentrated on the process of construction of knowledge, and on the importance of prior knowledge in learning and its contribution to increased achievement in science. A few of them investigated on students' epistemological beliefs, schema structure and development of curriculum and its implementation. The result of the reviewed studies indicated an improvement in achievement in science, science process skills and better attitude towards science as a result of constructivist approach. Many studies were conducted in physics and few had seen the impact on integrated science. Sporadically, studies were conducted on impact of constructivist approach on scientific attitude.

Along with the above results, it was also seen a clear understanding of concepts, long-term retention of knowledge acquired as a result to constructivist approach. Besides cognitive development, some of the studies revealed that constructivist approach is effective in developing confidence, self concept, certain social aspects like building good relationship among students and between student and teacher and so on.

Some of the studies concentrated on the construction of tools in the context of constructivist approach like Constructivist Learning Environment Survey scale, scientific attitude, TOUS etc.

In Indian context, research in the area of science education concentrated on designing science curriculum, experimentation of models of teaching in science, use of computers in science teaching and so on. Experimental studies were carried out to try out various models, methods and approaches in science. Number of correlation studies were conducted to examine the relationship among variables like achievement, attitudes, intelligence, gender and so on. Some of the studies were undertaken to assess the achievement level, and the attitudes of the students towards science.

As seen from the quantum of research studies carried out on constructivism in India, the insufficient research in this area is very prominent. Though there is an optimistic inclination towards constructivism seen in the National Curriculum Framework, 2005, followed by the preparation of textbooks based on Constructivist principles for classes III, VI, IX, XII (NCERT); the impact of the approach is yet to be studied empirically. This creates a need and a sufficient base or a rationale to carry out a research work to study the practicality of Constructivist approach in Indian classrooms.

The literature and the researches conducted in west provide innumerable cues to the present study, out of which, some of the findings like improvement in science achievement, process skills and Attitude towards science (Blunk and Yager, 1990; Kim, 1994; Sherri, 1995; Hyang-Lim, 1995; Brass and Duke, 1995; Banet and Nunez, 1997; Thomas, 1999; Pooran,2000; Shymansky, 2000; Terrance, 2001) as a result of Constructivist approach were considered. It was purported to study the constructivist approach on these variables in Indian classrooms to see if their effect would be similar to that of the studies reviewed.

In spite of certain variables been researched upon as an effect of constructivist approach, there are certain research gaps, which are obvious. For instance very few studies were found where in scientific attitude was considered as one of the consequence variables as an effect of constructivist approach (Preece and Baxter 2000), it is found that not all dimensions of scientific attitude were studied. They conducted a survey of the superstitions and pseudo scientific beliefs of the students. Reviewing upon the studies that were more limited in their scope, with respect to studying scientific attitude, the present study aimed to research upon the effect of constructivist approach on eight dimensions of scientific attitude in the context of Constructivist learning environment.

Though the present study draws certain cues and implications from the reviewed researches with respect to certain variables as mentioned above, it differs in certain purposes, which needs a specific mention. The study aimed to find out the effect of constructivist approach on the perception of students on the nature of science. It may be noted that there are very few studies conducted on knowing the epistemological beliefs of high school students (Adams, 1997; Blunck and Yager, 2000). Reflecting into the nature of science as a discipline and its ramification to science learning as a process, it is found inevitable to know the secondary level students' ideas and perceptions about the nature of science. It was found equally essential to study how constructivist approach affects students' learning science, which involve exploration, construction of knowledge, negotiation, sharing of ideas, scaffolding, analysis, synthesis, and reflective exercises shape the nature and understanding of science. Drawing the essential cues along with the research gaps identified from the review exercise carried out, the present study aims to explore upon the effect of constructivist approach on Achievement in science, Science Process Skills, Perception of Nature of Science, Scientific attitude and Attitude towards Science of secondary level students.

3

Methodology of the Study

This chapter deals with the different procedures followed in the construction and development of data gathering instruments on different variables which are included in the study, development of instructional materials and the methods adapted in selection of sample, collection of data, method of scoring and analysis.

Design of the Study

The present investigation was carried out to study the effectiveness of constructivist approach in learning of science. The design adopted in the study is quasi-experimental, which is different from true experimental designs in two ways. Firstly, the participants are not randomly selected from the specified population and secondly, the participants are not randomly assigned to experimental and control groups. Nevertheless, quasi-experimental designs provide a relatively high degree of experimental-control in natural settings and they clearly represent a step-up from pre-experimental designs because they enable the researchers to compare the performance of the experimental group with that of a control group. In other words, quasi-experimental designs enable researchers to move their experimentation out of the laboratory and into a natural setting or context (Martella, R.C., et al. Research Methods, 1999).

Nonequivalent control-group design was employed for the present study, which is similar to the pre-posttest control group design except for the absence of the random selection of the participants from a population and the random assignment of participants to groups. This design begins with the identification of naturally assembled experimental and control groups. The naturally occurring experimental and control groups should be as similar as possible and the assignment to one group or the other is assumed to be random. This design was found appropriate to be used in the present study in order to examine the effect of Constructivist approach on learners' learning of science in the natural setting without disturbing the classroom climate by either controlling or manipulating the variables.

Fig. 3.1: **Nonequivalent control group design**

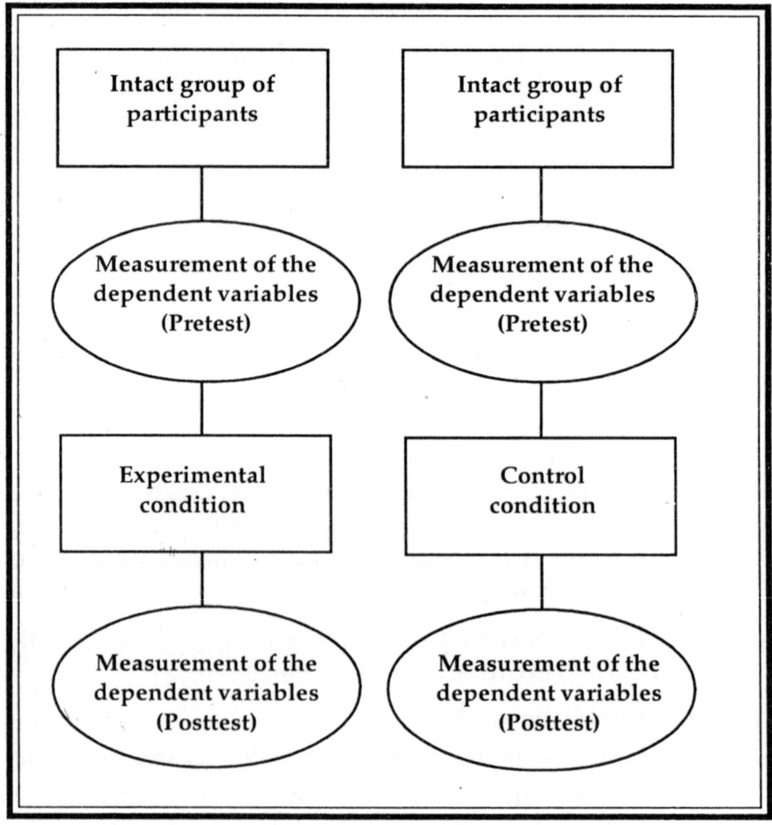

Moreover, this design takes care of the threats to internal validity i.e. maturation, selection, selection by maturation interaction, morality, instrumentation, testing, and history that result in changes in the performance of the experimental groups. The nonequivalent control group design does not control the statistical regression that can result in changes in the performance of the experiment group. The four threats to internal validity i.e. experimental treatment diffusion, compensatory rivalry by the control group and resentful demoralization of the control group that result in the changes in the performance of the control group are controlled by giving an equally desirable and alternative intervention to the control group students. The primary threat to the internal validity of this design is the possibility that differences on the post-test scores of experimental and control groups are the result of initial differences rather than the effects of the independent variable. Hence ANCOVA was used to control the initial difference between the experiment and control groups by adjusting the posttest means of the groups.

Sampling Procedure

The purposive sampling technique was employed to select the schools for the study, the details of which are as follows:

The two schools namely Demonstration Multipurpose School and Kendriya Vidyalaya situated in Mysore of Karnataka State were selected for the study as they both share demographic features such as

- ❖ Both the schools follow the CBSE syllabus (Central Board of Secondary Education) and the textbooks prepared by NCERT (National Council of Educational Research and Training).
- ❖ Both have same pattern of examination conducted by Central Board of Secondary Education.
- ❖ Both have similar infrastructure like well-equipped biology, chemistry and physics labs, activity rooms etc.
- ❖ Admission criteria and procedures followed in admitting the students is same in both the schools.

- Strength in each class is restricted to 35 in each section in both the schools.
- Students come from same socio-economic background, where most of the parents are the employees of the Central Government.
- Both the schools have trained Science graduate teachers. The recruitment of teachers is carried out by conducting tests in the particular subject area which is followed by interviews.
- The teachers in Kendriya Vidyalaya and Demonstration Multipurpose School are exposed to various innovative programmes conducted by NCERT related to new innovative methods of teaching, evaluation etc.

Demonstration Multipurpose School is a model school established by NCERT under Regional Institute of Education through out the country in order to try out the innovative programmes recommended for school education at National level. An institution of this kind provides more freedom and flexibility for trying out a new innovative method of teaching science when compared to other institutions. Hence this school was considered as Experimental group of which the eighth standard students of this school constitute the subjects for experimentation. The eighth standard students of Kendriya Vidyalaya were treated as the sample for control group of the study. In order to control the initial differences, as being quasi experimental design, the pretest scores of the tests along with the intelligence score were taken as covariates.

The eighth standard students of both schools were chosen as the sample because according to the cognitive development theory of Piaget (1977), the children of this age group i.e. 11 and above come under formal operation period. The children of this age group are capable of formal operations, i.e. are able to reason about the world not only through actions or single symbols, but also by figuring out the implications that are obtained among a set of related propositions. The child starts to use abstract reasoning. Abstract hypotheses can be built along with the capability to hold some variables constant while manipulating particular variables to determine its influence. In this period, the children learn to handle increasingly more and more complex logical operations. They have the potential to perform all those complex logical operations which are employed by scientists, mathematicians etc. like considering many alternatives to a problem; identify important variables that influence the outcomes of science activities and experiments; generate hypothesis; collect, organize and analyse data on their own. They are found to have the capacity to assimilate the old information with the newer ones and reconstruct the meanings when required. This was the main reason for selecting students of eight standard for experimentation.

Besides the above factor, it was easy to get permission and cooperation from the head master and the teachers for eighth standard when compared to ninth and tenth standards. The school authorities would not spare ninth and tenth standard students, as Secondary School Certificate examination serves as a turning point to their future, and students will be looking for better performance. Therefore, participation of students in the experiment would not be up to the expected level. Hence eighth standard was considered to be the suitable class from both the academic and administrative points of view for conducting the experiment.

Sample for the Study

The intact groups of sixty-eight eighth standard students in total including both experimental and control group were taken up for the study. The sample included 37 boys and 31 girls in total.

Table 3.1: Sample for the study

Sample	Boys	Girls	Total
Experimental group	21	15	36
Control group	16	16	32
Total	**37**	**31**	**68**

The experimental group (Demonstration Multipurpose School) consisted of 36 eighth standard students, of which were 21 boys and 15 girls and the control group (Kendriya Vidyalaya, Mysore) consisted of 32 eighth standard students, which included 16 boys and 16 girls.

Selection of Content

The science subject of eighth standard was chosen to teach through constructivist approach. The eighth standard science textbook consisted of fifteen units, among which seven units were chosen (i.e. 50%) that included two chemistry, two physics and three biology units. The units selected have interrelated concepts, which aided the students in learning new concepts. The units chosen were as follows:

1. Conservation of natural resources
2. Metals and their properties
3. Electric current
4. Magnetism
5. Pressure
6. Organic evolution, and
7. How leaves are designed?

Procedural Details of the Study

The study was carried out in three phases.

Phase I - Developmental Phase

At this stage, the investigator developed instructional materials including lesson plans, activity sheets, unit tests and tools namely achievement test in science, perception of nature of science test, science process skills test, scientific attitude scale, attitude towards science scale and a reaction scale.

Development of the Lessons Based on Constructivist Model

After the selection of the content the investigator carried out the following tasks:

(i) Content Analysis

The content selected from eighth standard science textbook was analyzed to identify science concepts, teaching points, science process skills, attitudes, skills and values. The content was reorganized in order to have continuity, sequence and integration of learning experiences wherever required. The content analysis is summarized in the following format and an illustration of one unit is presented in the following table:

Table 3.2: **Content analysis of unit magnetism**

Unit	Major Concepts/Teaching points	Process skills	Attitudes
Magnetism	1. **Magnet and its characteristics**	Observing, hypothesizing, prediciting, inferring	Curiosity, understands the discovery of magnet, intellectual honesty, rationality, free from superstitions
	2. **Magnetic and non-magnetic substances**	Observing, classifying, differentiating, hypothesizing	Open mindedness, willingness to suspend judgements
	3. **Types of magnet**	Observing, identifying, reasoning, inferring	Appreciates the magnetic power
	4. **Magnetic induction**	Observing, hypothesising predicting, inferring, generalization, interpretation	Rationality, perseverance, open mindedness
	5. **Electromagnet**	Observing, hypothesizing inferring	Perseverance, open mindedness
	6. **Demagnetization**	Observing, reasoning, seeing cause and effect relationship	Free from superstitions, rationality
	7. **Uses of magnet**	Observing	Rationality, willingness to suspend judgement

(ii) Planning of Lessons

According to American Association of the Advancement of Science (AAAS, 1990), National Science Education Standards (NSES, 1996) and National Curricular Framework for School

Education (NFSE, 2000) the major objectives of science education include experiencing science as inquiry, understanding the interrelationships of science and technology; using personal and social perspectives to understand science; comprehending the nature of science throughout its history and building favourable science attitudes and achieving scientific literacy. Keeping all the objectives in mind, the lessons were planned using 4Es model.

(iii) Planning and Learning Model: 4Es

The planning model presented below is adapted from Science Curriculum Improvement Study (1962). It was made use of with some modifications in the present study. This model uses a conceptual focus that helps the learners to construct meaning, encourages students to expand understanding of that fundamental meaning, and evaluates student performance in authentic ways. This format is credited with the greatest student achievement gains in major research studies and significant improvements in student science attitudes and inquiry skills, when compared to similar experiential science programmes and traditional science curricula (Shymansky et al., 1982; Bredderman, 1982).

Firstly, the concepts to be learnt were identified and the learning activity was structured accordingly. This approach included 4Es: exploration, explanation, expansion and evaluation. The four steps along with an example are given below.

Fig. 3.2: **The planning and learning cycle**

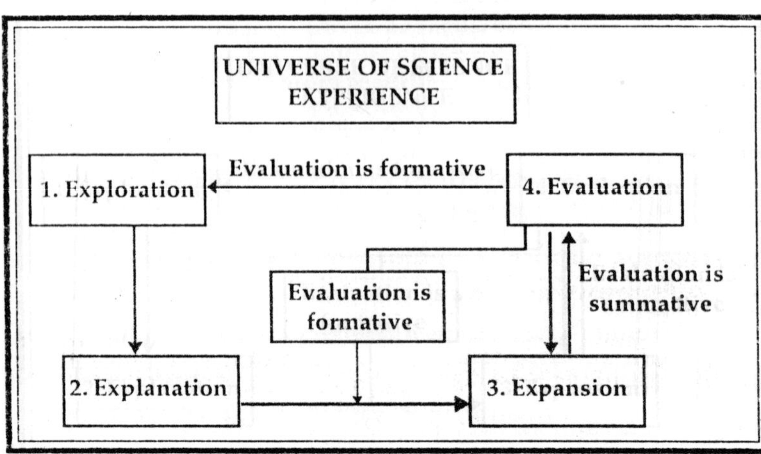

Step I. Planning for Student Exploration

Children were provided concrete materials and experiences and the following questions help in planning for this stage of exploration:

- What do I want the children to learn? (goals, objectives, attitudes, processes and products)
- What concepts will be invented? (science products)
- What activities must the children do to find and to construct the needed data? (processes, information, answers to question)
- What kind of records should the children keep? (process skills)
- What kind of instructions and encouragement will the children need? (attitudes)

At this stage the teachers need to direct the activities of children and suggest what kinds of records they should keep. They should not tell or explain the concept. This step should be planned carefully, so that it becomes student centered and student-activity based.

Example 1

Objectives to be Attained

The students are expected to:

(a) differentiate magnetic and non-magnetic substances.

(b) understand how domains of iron differ from a magnet.

Concepts to be Learnt

Magnet

Additional Concepts that are Important for Expansion

Magnetic substances, non-magnetic substances, domains of a magnet.

Strategy Used

Experimentation, Concept attainment game.

Process Skills to be Developed

Observing, identifying, classifying, experimenting, hypothesizing, inferring, drawing.

Attitudes to be Developed

Understand the history of magnet and appreciate its power, curiosity, open-mindedness and cooperation.

Stage of Exploration

What will the students do? Teachers instructions to the students: " Here are some substances and a wonderful rock, try to classify the substances into two groups. Once you classified them, try to name and define them, and also write the properties of the wonderful rock."

Children observe, feel and experiment with the materials given to them.

St1: Hey, let me see this wonderful rock.

St2: Why did madam call it as wonderful rock? (curiosity)

St1: May be....

(Suddenly, the students see that the rock attracted the metal pieces)

St1: Yes, it is a magnet.

St4: How do you know that it is a magnet?

St1: See here, it is attracting the metal pieces.

St5: and St6: (also tries and found that it is not attracting sand and chalk piece.)

Why is it like this? (Experimenting with other objects)

St3: May be it is having some unnatural power. (hypothesising)

St10: I don't think so.

St1: May be it attracts only metals. (hypothesising)

St12: But see here it is not attracting gold.

(Students in the group separated the materials, which are attracted by the magnet from others. They cross checked with each other.)

Tr: Which substances does the magnet attract?

(Students list the substances like iron nail, pins etc. that are attracted by the magnet.)

Tr: All of you have seen a magnet, do you know who and how it was discovered?

St9: I know the story of discovery of a magnet. Five thousand years ago people of Magnesia discovered that a particular rock could attract small pieces of iron towards it incidentally. Then it was named as Magnetite. Chinese called them as lodestone. (History of science)

St4: That's great. (Appreciation)

St5: You know our earth is also like a magnet.

St7: Yes. Any thing thrown up falls down. i.e. it attracts every object towards itself.

St9: It is gravitational pull.

Step II. Planning for Explanation

The main purpose of this phase was to reach mental equilibrium through accommodation, as described in the theory of Piaget (1977). Equilibrium is reached when a new concept is formed and linked to previously understood concepts. Here, students must focus on their primary findings from exploration, and the teacher helps the students by introducing proper language or concept labels. This step was originally called concept invention. The teacher's task is to lead the students through a discussion, so that students discover the concept by inventing it for themselves.

The teacher's technique is to question skillfully so that the students use the experiences of their explorations to construct scientific meaning. The following questions will help the teacher in planning for the stage of explanation:

- What kind of information or findings are students expected to provide? (products, process skills)
- How will the students' findings from the exploration phase be reviewed and summarized? (Teacher questioning, pupil discussion, graphing, board work)
- How can I use the findings of students and refrain from telling them what they should have found even if they are incorrect or incomplete? (Teacher questioning, guided construction, attitudes)
- What are the proper concept labels or terms that must be attached to the concept? (Products)
- What reason can I give the students if they ask me why the concept is important? (Teacher exposition, lesson expansion) This question automatically leads to the next phase: Expansion

  Teacher asks the name of the concept.

Concept: Magnet

Using the students own ideas and words, the teacher helped, constructed and explained that magnet is a rock which attracts some of the metal pieces and its power was found to be more at the edges. The teacher showed the students that the magnet mainly attracted the substances made of iron. A key question used by the teacher "Which are the regions where the magnetic power is high"? There were two answers—north and south edges. The teacher replaced the word edges by poles.

Step III. Planning for Expansion

The purpose of this phase was to help students organize their thinking by applying what they have just learnt through their experiences that are related to the concepts of the selected lesson and to help the students to expand their ideas. The following questions would help in the maximum student involvement in the class:

- What previous experiences did the children have that are related to the concept? How can I connect the concept to these experiences? (New activities, questioning)

- ❖ Give some examples of how the concept and the activities encourage the student's science inquiry skills? (Learning activities, questioning)
- ❖ What examples can be used to illustrate the interrelationship of science and technology and the contributions of each to the society and quality of life? (Discussion, readings, uses of multimedia, class projects)
- ❖ Give some examples to show how science has influenced our society, policies and laws? (Linkages with social studies, current events)
- ❖ What new experiences do the children need in order to expand on the concept? (Processes, attitudes, activities)
- ❖ What is the next concept related to the present one? How can I encourage exploration of the next concept? (Products, processes)

How will the concept of magnet be applied and expanded?

Tr: We have seen that magnet attracts some substances and does not attract some.

Can you give a term for the substances, which are attracted by a magnet?

St2: Magnetic substances.

St7: The substances, which are not attracted by the magnet, can be called non-magnetic substances.

St3: North and south poles attract and north and north poles move away from each other.

St4: Like poles attract and unlike poles go away.

Tr: Restructures the statement as "Like poles repel and unlike poles attract".

(Students repeat the statement given by the teacher).

Tr: Do you know why the magnets attract substances made of iron?

St1: I think molecules of iron might have magnetic properties. (Hypothesising)

Tr: Very good. You are correct. Iron has magnetic properties.

Teacher gives explanation with the help of a diagram showing the domains in iron rod and that of the magnet and explains how magnet attracts the iron pieces.

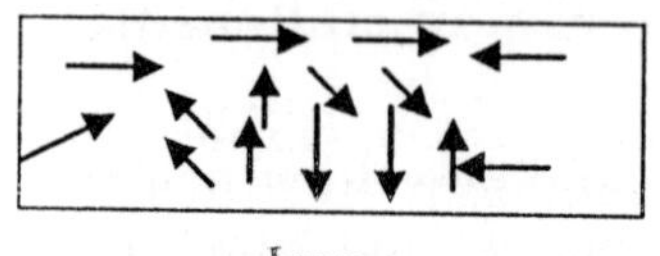

Iron

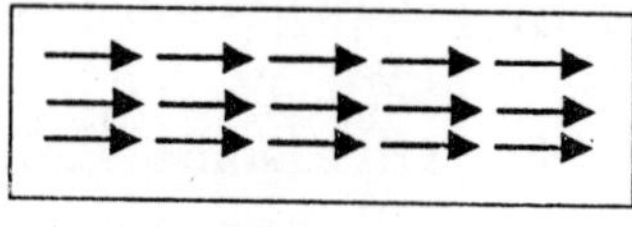

Magnet

As you are aware of, every substance is made up of molecules. We call them small units or domains. In the same way, iron is also made of molecules, which move in a random way. Whereas, in the case of a magnet they move in one particular direction either from north to south or from south to north.

When a magnet is subjected towards an iron substance, all the domains of iron change their direction towards the magnet. Thus the iron substance gets attracted towards magnet.

Tr: Well, we have learnt the nature of magnet till now. Do you know, where do we use magnets in our daily life?

St4: Toys.

Tr: Do you know, how cranes lift heavy loads?

St: No.

Tr: Big magnets are made use of in the cranes for lifting heavy loads.

St: We can separate iron pieces from non-magnetic substances with the help of a magnet.

St7: It is having such a great power of attraction. That's really wonderful. (appreciates)

Tr: It is so useful to mankind. Thanks to science and technology that brought the magnets into use in many fields like medicine, extraction of metals etc.

(The students appreciate the usefulness of magnets and the technology of make use of it in a variety of purposes)

Step IV. Planning for Evaluation

The purpose of this phase was to go beyond standard forms of testing. Consistent evaluation can help to reveal misconceptions before they become deeply rooted. Certain questions were kept in mind like,

- What key questions should I ask to encourage deep exploration? (processes, attitudes)
- What questions can I ask to help students think about their data in an effort to construct realistic concepts? (processes)
- What hands-on assessments can the students do to demonstrate the basic skills of observation, classification, communication, measurement, prediction and inference? (processes)
- What reflective questions assessment will indicate how well the students recall and use what has been learned? (products)

The teacher gives a prediction sheet containing different substances; the students were asked to classify them into magnetic and non-magnetic substances.

Tr: O.k. students, you have identified magnetic and non-magnetic substances with the help of a magnet. Can you show me the poles of a magnet and explain how it attracts ferrous substances.

(Students explain the attractive power of a magnet.)

Tr: Good.

Teacher draws a concept map showing the properties of magnet and its types with the help of students.

Fig. 3.3: **Magnet and its properties**

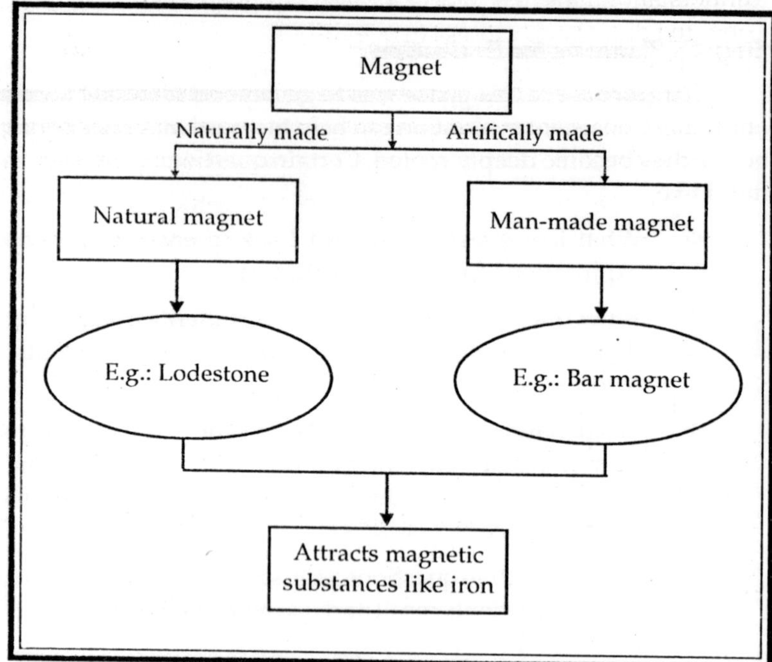

Tr: Asks a pupil to explain the concept and properties of magnet seeing the concept map.

Tr: Did you all enjoy drawing this concept map?

St: Yes.

Tr: Very good.

Now the students were asked to explore and find out some more objects from their daily life that are magnetic in nature. Thus the cycle of 4E's continues.

As discussed in the chapter I, in constructivist view, learning cannot be separated from action. Perception and action work together in a dialogical manner. Thus, the lessons were structured in such a way that the students had an opportunity to get directly involved with the phenomena and materials. They had the oppurtunity to explain, expand and elaborate the concepts learnt, make connections to other related concepts and apply their understandings to the world around them. The last phase is an ongoing diagnostic process that allows the teacher to determine if the learner has attained understanding of concepts and knowledge. Evaluation and assessment occur at all points along the continuum of the instructional process. Thus, the teacher is just a facilitator, providing materials and guiding the students' focus. The hands on assignments, work sheets, daily assignments, project works, unit tests were developed along with the lesson plans for all the selected units. The unit tests included a variety of test items like Multiple choice type items, Fill in the blanks, Classification type, Reflective questioning, Concept maps both filling gaps and description, and so on.

Phase II-Try Out of the Lessons

Three lessons namely Light, Metals and their properties, Adaptations and organic evolution were selected for the pilot study and were tried out in one of the local schools following the CBSE syllabus. The instructional materials developed were tried out on 34 students belonging to eighth standard of JSS Public School, J.P. Nagar, Mysore. The units were taught using the constructivist approach for a period of two months. Unit tests were conducted after the completion of a unit. Classes were audio recorded for continuous feedback to the investigator and modifications were made accordingly.

Tools Used/Developed in the Study

To study the effectiveness of constructivist approach on the dependent variables, various tools were used. The following table gives the details of the tools and the purpose for which they were used.

The description of all the above tools are given below.

(i) Ravens Progressive Matrices

Ravens progressive matrices was used to know the mental ability of the students. The test is made up of five sets of diagrammatic puzzles exhibiting serial changes in two dimensions simultaneously. Each puzzle has a part missing, which the person taking the test has to find among the options provided.

Table 3.3: Tools used and their purpose

Sl. No.	Name of the tool used	Author	Variable measured
1.	Ravens progressive matrices	Raven J.C.	Intelligence
2.	Achievement test in science	Investigator	Pretest and post-test levels on science achievement
3.	Perception of nature of science test	Investigator	Pretest and post-test levels on perception of nature of science
4.	Science process skills test	Investigator	Pretest and post-test levels on science process skills
5.	Scientific attitude scale	Investigator	Pretest and post-test levels on scientific attitude
6.	Attitude towards science scale	Investigator	Pretest and post-test levels on attitude towards science
7.	Reaction scale	Investigator	Reactions of students on constructivist approach

The standard test consists of sixty problems divided into five sets (A, B, C, D, and E) each made up of 12 problems. In each set the first problem is as nearly as possible self-evident. The problems, which follow, build on the argument of those that have gone before and become progressively more difficult. It was designed in such a way that it can be used with children as well as adults.

The test-retest reliabilities reported by the authors Stinissen, Dolke, Sheppart and Goetzinger, range from 0.80 to 0.93 and Internal consistency reliabilities reported, range from 0.87 to 0.97 (Blansk and Sinha, Elley and Mac Arthur King, Laroche and Bruke).

It was found to have a high predictive validity with scholastic achievement (0.70) and the correlation of Standard Progressive Matrices with Binet and Wescheler scale range from 0.54 to 0.86. The progressive matrix has been described as one of the purest and best of the available measures of general intellectual functioning ('g'). Factor analytic studies reveal high loading up to 0.83 on 'g' factor.

In the present study, the test was administered to both the experimental and control groups in the pretest stage. The students were asked to answer in the response sheets provided to them.

Scoring

The investigator scored the test manually using the scoring key as given in the manual of RPM. Each correct answer was given one mark. The total raw score was found and was taken as a covariate in the present study.

Construction and Validation of Tools

Even though there were many standardized tests available, it was felt necessary to construct the tools, as the study intended to examine the effectiveness of constructivist approach. The tests already prepared differed in the content, context, sample for which they have to be used and so on. Thus, there was a need to construct the tools on these angles. Since tests and instruments are relative in nature, the norms developed on a certain test can only be cautiously employed for investigating another problem. Specificity of instruments therefore, can be best maintained if new instrument consistent with the aims and objectives of the research are developed. Cronbach (1964) stated that a test, which helps in making one decision in a particular research situation, may have no value at all for another. So the investigator constructed the above tools.

(ii) Achievement Test in Science

To test the pre- and post- achievement levels of students of experimental and control groups, this test was designed by the investigator. The details of construction of achievement test in science is as follows:

During the preparation of lesson plans, the concepts, teaching points and respective objectives were listed out. Objectives emphasizing knowledge, understanding, application and skill levels were framed for all the selected units. Blooms taxonomy was made use of while writing the objectives.

Item Pooling

The items were pooled based on the objectives framed. Appropriate weightages were given to the various types of objectives, content and the type of questions. The assessment was objective based and the test planned included objective type test items like multiple choice items, fill in the blanks, classification type items, identifying and descriptive questions like short answered type questions.

The test items thus framed were further scrutinized and edited by the investigator from the point of view of language suitability, ambiguity and for their correspondence to specific behavioural outcomes and comprehensibility. The content validity of the test was obtained by giving it to experts from Demonstration Public School and Regional institute of Education, Mysore. They scrutinized and studied the items of the test in terms of their sampling individual units and ensuring coverage of behavioural objectives comprising of knowledge, understanding, application and skill. On the basis of their suggestions, appropriate modifications were made and a total number of sixty items were selected for achievement test.

The test items were arranged in such a way that the similar kind of items appeared together and care was taken to see that each set of items was preceded by specific instructions as to how the learner would have to respond to the set of items. The total time allotted to answer the test was 60 minutes. The scoring procedure and marking scheme was prepared.

Try Out of the Test

The test items were subjected to a formal try out on a sample of 100 students of eighth standard from the local schools of Mysore city. Item analysis was performed in order to identify weak or defective items to make further improvement; identify ambiguous and intermediate implausible distracters; very difficult and very easy items; determine the difficulty level of each individual test item and lastly to determine the number of test items to be included in the final test. A schedule was drawn after having a consultation with the principals of the selected institutions. The students were asked to sit comfortably and were told the purpose of the administration of the test. They were given both general and specific instructions regarding the test and were asked to answer the items in the question paper itself. All the precautionary measures were taken to avoid mutual help and to avoid unfair means in answering the questions. The average time taken by the students to answer the achievement test was found to be one hour.

Item Analysis of the Test

The answer scripts were corrected with the help of scoring key prepared. Item analysis was carried out to find out the difficulty value and discriminative index, as the test was content oriented. Among the various procedures of item analysis the method advocated by Ebel (1966) in the book "Measuring Educational Achievement" was followed. The following steps were taken up in the process of item analysis:

- Firstly the scored test papers or answer sheets were arranged in ascending or descending order.
- Then the two sub-groups of test papers i.e. upper 27 percent (students received highest marks) and the lower 27 percent (students received lowest marks) of the groups were separated.

- The frequency of each possible response to each item for the chosen groups was found out.
- The sum of the frequencies for the two groups was calculated and then item difficulty and discriminative index were found for each item with the help of the formulae given below:

$$D.V. = \frac{R(high) + R(low)}{2N} \times 100$$ **Difficulty value**

$$D.P. = \frac{R(high) - R(low)}{N}$$ **Disciminative power**

where R (high) = number of correct responses to an item in the high group

R (low) = number of correct responses to an item in the low group

N = 27% of the total group.

The result of item analysis of the items in the science achievement test is as follows:

Table 3.4: Item analysis of achievement test in science

Item No.	High	Low	D.V	D.P
1	2	3	4	5
I1	12	5	53	0.44
2	16	8	75	0.5
3	14	9	72	0.31
4	14	9	72	0.31
5	9	3	37	0.37
6	16	7	72	0.56
7	16	8	75	0.5
8	15	9	75	0.37
9	7	2	45	0.31
10	12	4	50	0.5
11	16	6	69	0.62

(Contd...)

1	2	3	4	5
12	8	2	31	0.37
13	10	2	37	0.5
14	16	7	72	0.56
15	15	7	69	0.5
16	13	8	66	0.31
17	14	4	56	0.62
18	11	3	44	0.5
19	8	2	31	0.37
20	12	6	56	0.37
21	6	2	25	0.25
22	15	7	69	0.5
23	13	8	66	0.31
24	15	9	75	0.37
25	12	5	53	0.44
26	12	4	50	0.5
27	12	4	50	0.5
28	14	7	66	0.44
29	13	4	53	0.56
30	13	5	56	0.5
31	14	5	59	0.56
32	14	5	59	0.56
33	14	8	69	0.37
34	14	9	72	0.31
35	10	2	37	0.5
36	7	1	25	0.37
II37	16	9	78	0.44
38	8	2	31	0.37
39	12	5	53	0.44
40	13	4	53	0.56
41	8	4	37	0.25
42	8	2	31	0.37
43	12	8	62	0.25

(Contd...)

1	2	3	4	5
44	15	9	75	0.37
III45	16	8	75	0.5
46	16	6	68	0.62
47	10	3	40	0.44
48	12	5	53	0.44
49	9	3	37	0.37
50	8	4	37	0.25
51	10	6	50	0.25
52	8	4	37	0.25
53	14	9	72	0.31
54	8	4	37	0.25
55	14	4	56	0.62
56	13	8	66	0.31
57	6	2	25	0.25
58	13	8	66	0.31
59	14	7	66	0.44
60	6	2	25	0.25

Item Selection

As suggested by Noll et al. (1965), the items with a difficulty value in the range of 21-80% and discriminating power greater than 0.20 were selected for the final test, which amounted to sixty items. No items were deleted from the test developed as a result of item analysis.

Reliability of the Test

The reliability of the test is its ability to yield consistent result from one set of measures to another. It has two closely related connotations in psychological testing i.e. to examine to what extent a test is internally consistent and to what extent the test yields consistent result upon testing and retesting. The test-retest reliability method was carried out in the present study to find out the reliability of all the tools.

The achievement test in science was administered twice, leaving a gap of one month in between the tests. The two sets of scores were correlated to obtain the reliability of the test. A high positive correlation (r = 0.90) was found which indicated the high reliability of the achievement test.

The correlation coefficient values of all the tests constructed were tabulated in Table 3.17.

Final Form of the Test

The final form of the achievement test consisted of 60 items, including 36 Multiple-choice items, 8 Fill in the blanks and 16 Short answer questions with the allocation of sixty marks on the whole test.

The weightages given to objectives in the test were as follows:

Table 3.5: Weightage given to the objectives

Sl.No.	Type of objective	No. of items	Marks allotted	Percentage
1.	Knowledge	13	9½	16
2.	Understanding	36	36½	61
3.	Application	9	11	18
4.	Skill	2	3	5
	Total	60	60	100

Table 3.5 shows the emphasis of understanding and application level items in the test. From the above table it is clear that 61% (36½) of the total marks were items which measured the comprehension ability of the students. Nine items with eleven marks i.e. 18% of the total marks were included which would measured the application level of students.

Table 3.6: Weightage to the content

Sl. No.	Content	No. of items	Marks allotted	Percentage
1.	Conservation of natural resources	12	10½	18
2.	Metals and their properties	6	5	8
3.	Electric current	14	15	25
4.	Pressure	6	6	10
5.	Magnetism	6	5½	9
6.	Organic evolution	9	11	18
7.	How leaves are designed?	7	7	12
	Total	**60**	**60**	**100**

From the above table, it is clear that units like 'Conservation of natural resources' and 'Electric current' were given more weightage in the test. The remaining units were given approximately equal weightage. The items were based on the constructivist means of evaluation. Totally sixty items of various types were included as indicated in the table below:

Table 3.7: Weightage given to the type of questions

Sl.No.	Type of items	No. of items	Marks allotted	Percentage
1.	Multiple choice	36	18	30
2.	Fill in the blanks	8	8	13
3.	Short answered questions	16	34	57
	Total	**60**	**60**	**100**

Table 3.7 shows that Multiple choice type items were allotted 30% of the total marks i.e. Multiple choice items carried 18 marks, Short answer items carried 34 marks which is 57% of the total test marks. The short answer questions included classification type items and application level items, which measured the comprehension and application ability of the students.

Keeping the weightages in mind, a blue print was made.

Blue Print for the Test

A blue print balancing different objectives, content units, type of items, was prepared and followed for the purpose of building in curricular validity at all stages of the compilation of the whole test.

Table 3.8: Blue print for the achievement test in science

Sl. No.	Content	Knowledge			Understanding			Application			Skill			Marks
		M	F	S	M	F	S	M	F	S	M	F	S	
1.	Conservation of natural resources	4 (½)	1(1)		6 (½)		1(2) 1(3)							13 (11)
2.	Metals and their properties	1(½)	1(1)		3 (½)		1(2)							6(5)
3.	Electric current		1(1)		2 (½)		1(2)	5 ½)		1(4) 1(1)			1(2) 1(1)	13 (14½)
4.	Pressure				3 (½)		1(1)	1 (½)		1(3)				6(6)
5.	Magnetism		1(1)		3 (½)	1(1)	1(2)							6 (5½)
6.	Organic evolution	2(½)	2(1)		2 (½)		2(2) 1(3)							9(11)
7.	How leaves are designed?				4 (½)	1(1)	2(2)							7(7)
	Total	7(3½)	6(6)		23(11½)	2(2)	11(23)	6(3)		3(8)			2(3)	60(60)

* **Number inside the bracket indicates the marks allotted.**

* **Number outside the bracket indicates number of questions.**

The items were arranged type-wise and in the increasing order of difficulty level with specific instructions. A few examples of test items along with objectives to be attained from the test are given in the following table.

Table 3.9: Examples of test items from the achievement test in science

Sl. No.	Category	General description	Examples of the test items
1.	Knowledge recalls, names, defines, states	Recalls the full form of WWF defines **adaptation**	1. WWF stands for ____________. 2. The development of characteristics that help an organism to survive in a particular environment is known as ____________________.
2.	Understanding explains, classifies, reasons out, differentiates, sees relationship	Classifies substances into conductors and insulators Reasons out why aluminium vessels turn dull grey after use	1. Classify the following substances into conductors and insulators silver, tap water, ebonite rod, human body, pure water, mica, gold, plastics. 2. Why does aluminium vessels become dull grey very soon after use?

(Contd...)

Sl. No.	Category	General description	Examples of the test items
3.	Application solve, illustrate, calculate shows	Illustrates the application of pressure. applies the principle "greater the area, greater the heat produced"	1. List out applications of pressure in your daily life. 2. You are given an electric stove and coils of different lengths, which among them would you, use to get more heat? a. longest coil b. shortest coil c. medium sized coil d. any of the above
4.	Skill Draws, computes	Draws a complete circuit	1. You are given three cells and one bulb. How will you connect them and glow the bulb? Draw the circuit diagram.

(iii) Perception of Nature of Science Test

Perception of nature of science test was developed to know the perceptions of students on nature of science. Nature of science is most commonly referred to the values and assumptions inherent to scientific knowledge. It was found that students' conceptions of nature of science influence their thoughts, feelings and actions associated with doing and understanding of science. Evidence suggests that knowledge of nature of science assists students' learning of science content. Driver (1991) also insisted on inclusion of nature of science as a goal of instruction as it supports successful learning of science content. Nature of science also enhances interest in science and decision-making ability among the students. Many researchers have developed the tool that measures the perception of nature of science for pre-service teachers (TOUS—Test for understanding of science), whereas there is no tool developed for secondary school children that too in Indian context. So the investigator felt that there was a need to develop a tool to know the perceptions of students on nature of science.

In the present study, perception of nature of science by students pertains to the following aspects:

- Characteristics of Science
- Scientific methods/processes
- Use of scientific discoveries
- Application of science in daily life
- Role of science in society and its impact on human beings.

Item Pooling

The items were written based on the above five components. The items included both objective as well as descriptive questions. Twenty-five multiple choice type items and five open ended questions were written in the preliminary form of the test with space for pupils responses. Each item carried one mark and the open-ended questions were given ten marks. Both the general as well as specific instructions were given to the students.

Try Out and Item Analysis

The items were subjected to try out on sixty eighth standard students of local schools of Mysore city and item analysis was done on similar lines as that of science achievement test. The result of item analysis of perception of nature of science test is given in the following table:

Table 3.10: Item analysis of perception of nature of science test

Item No.	High	Low	D.V.	D.P.
1.	16	7	63.88	0.50
2.	16	8	66.66	0.44
3.	15	10	69.44	0.27
4.	12	7	52.77	0.27
5.	13	4	47.22	0.50
6.	14	8	61.11	0.33
7.	12	6	50.00	0.33
8.	17	11	77.77	0.33
9.	18	10	77.77	0.44
10.	15	4	52.77	0.61
11.	16	10	72.00	0.33
12.	16	8	66.66	0.44
13.	14	16	83.33	0.22
14.	15	10	69.44	0.27
15.	15	4	52.77	0.61
16.	18	11	40.27	0.38
17.	17	12	80.00	0.27
18.	15	7	61.00	0.44
19.	16	10	72.00	0.33
20.	10	2	33.33	0.44
21.	16	8	66.66	0.44
22.	17	18	97.00	0.05*
23.	17	4	58.33	0.72
24.	15	10	69.44	0.27
25.	15	9	66.66	0.33

(Contd...)

Item No.	High	Low	D.V	D.P
26.	18	3	58.33	0.83
27.	17	10	75.00	0.38
28.	15	16	86.00*	0.05*
29.	7	0	19.44*	0.38
30.	15	3	50.00	0.66

* Items deleted from the study.

Final Form of the Test

Four items were deleted for the final test as suggested by Noll et al. (1965), among them two items (Item numbers twenty-two and twenty eight) could not differentiate low achievers and high achievers and it was found that twenty-eighth item was too easy and twenty-ninth item was too difficult. On the whole twenty-six items were included in the perception of nature of science test. Overall, the test was of thirty marks.

Reliability of the Test

The reliability of the test was studied by administering the test on two different occasions to the same sample of pupils with a gap of thirty days in between. Through the analysis, it was found that the correlation coefficient was ($r = 0.70$) which indicated the high reliability of the test.

(iv) Science Process Skills Test

As mentioned earlier, science is a process as well as a product both complementing each other. In general, science process skills refer to the cognitive processes or thinking processes in which the learner is engaged while learning science. The exercise of these process skills generates the products of learning science—meaning, definition, explanation of terms, concepts, principles, laws, theories etc. American Association for the Advancement of Science, (1990) in the programme "Science—A Process Approach" emphasized the development of science process skills among all the levels of children. Science process skills were defined as broadly transferable, appropriate to many science disciplines and reflective of the true behaviours of scientists. When a child taking a role of a scientist interacts with physical and biological world around him, he observes, questions, plans, hypothesizes, infers, interprets etc. which in turn lead to construction of scientific knowledge. As the constructivist approach is more of activity oriented and child centered, where in the child explores the environment on his own in the present study, it was intended to assess the science process skills developed among the students of eighth standard. Thus the investigator decided to develop a science process skills test.

Selection of Science Process Skills

The main considerations in the selection of science processes for the present study were the following:

1. The processes must be appropriate for the eighth grade students of 12-14 years and their appropriateness must have some psychological base.
2. The processes selected must be emphasized in the objectives of the science curriculum followed by the eighth standard students of the selected schools.
3. The processes selected must be validated in some prior study for a similar population.
4. The processes selected must be capable of evaluation through an objective paper-pencil test.

From the review of relevant literature, the investigator found the paradigm of science processes, enunciated by Tannenbaum (1968) in his study related with the measurement of science processes of junior high school (grades seventh, eighth, ninth) of American schools, most appropriate. The processes validated by Tannenbaum were observing, comparing, classifying, quantifying, measuring, experimenting, inferring and predicting. Of these, observing, comparing, classifying, measuring and experimenting were considered as the concrete science process skills and quantifying, predicting were considered as the abstract science process skills.

For the present study, observing, inferring, predicting, hypothesizing, and interpreting were taken up. In constructivist approach, the misconceptions of the students are found out and the students reconstruct their experiences in their own way through constructive work. During this process they learn to reason out their experiences. With this perspective, reasoning was also included as one of the process skills of science.

(a) Observing

It is the primary way children obtain information. Observation causes identifying object properties or identifying changes in various physical systems through similarities and differences. An example of an observation could be: The object is hard, grey, round and the size of a baseball. The indicators of assessing observing skill are:

1. Making use of several senses
2. Noticing relevant details of the surroundings
3. Identifying similarities and differences
4. Discerning the order in which events take place
5. Using aids to the senses for study of details

E.g.: 1. When do you see a rainbow?

2. Our clothes dry faster when the weather is ___________.

(b) Reasoning

Reasoning is the mental process of finding the possible cause of a particular observation or incident.

E.g.: 1. Why thunderclap follows the lightening flash?

(c) Inferring

Inferences are conclusions about the cause of an observation. In the present study, inferring is the mental process a person goes through which he observes facts and tries to explain what they mean.

E.g.: 1. Every morning the sun appears to rise and set in the evening because of___________.

(d) Predicting

Predictions refer to types of thinking that require our best guesses based on the information available to us. Based on the obtained data and previous information, students predict a particular event by recognizing the underlying phenomena. Meteorologists, for example, predict the weather. Their predictions are made in advance of the weathers actual occurrence and are based on accumulated observations, analysis of information and prior experience. The indicators for predicting skill are:

1. Making use of evidence from past or present experience in stating what may happen
2. Explicitly using pattern in evidence to extrapolate or interpolate
3. Justifying a statement about what will happen or be found in terms of present evidence or past experiences
4. Showing caution in making assumptions about a pattern applying beyond the range of evidence
5. Distinguishing a prediction from a guess.

E.g.:

1. What will be the resultant force if two equal and opposite forces act at a point?
2. A body completely dipped in water, the weight of the water displaced by the body will be

(e) Interpreting

Given the data, the students interpret in their own way. Interpreting data requires the student to collect the observations and measurements in an organized way and draw conclusions from the information obtained by reading tables, graphs and diagrams. Indicators for interpreting include:

1. Finding patterns or trends in observations or results of investigations
2. Identifying an association between one variable and other
3. Making sure that a pattern or association is checked against the data

E.g.: The table below gives the number of dropouts in a school for a period of ten years. Comment on it.

(f) Hypothesizing

It is the mental process whereby an individual makes a guess about what will happen if the conditions in experimental situations are altered. It requires greater mental operations since the children do not see the experimental situation and have to picture them mentally. Indicators of hypothesizing are:

1. Suggesting an explanation which is consistent with the evidence
2. Suggesting an explanation which is consistent with some scientific principle and concept
3. Applying previous knowledge in attempting an explanation
4. Realizing that there can be more than one possible explanation of an event or phenomenon
5. Realizing tentative nature of any explanation.

E.g.:

1. What do you think will happen when water is poured into the carton box with number of holes which were I centimeter apart?
2. What do you think will happen when sugar is heated?

It was decided to have a content-based process skills test. Firstly, the concepts from seventh and eighth standard science syllabus were listed out. Then objectives were framed with respect to the above science process skills. The test item (assessing the science process skills) is either in the form of a question or statement with four alternatives. The students were expected to tick one of the alternatives given.

Item Pooling

The items were written in the form of multiple choice on the selected process skills, keeping in mind the age, mental ability and grade of the students. They were discussed with subject experts to get their feedback regarding—the inclusion of those items under specific process skills, their suitability to the age group and their mental ability. In the light of the feedback, they were modified accordingly.

Try Out and Item Analysis of the Test

The items thus prepared were tried out on a sample of 100 students of eighth standard of local schools. Each correct answer was given one mark. The answers were scored and item analysis was done to find out the difficulty value and discriminative index of every item. The results of item analysis are tabulated below:

Table 3.11: Item analysis of science process skills test

Item No.	High	Low	D.V.	D.P.
1.	17	8	46.30	0.33
2.	9	7	29.60	0.07*
3.	19	12	57.40	0.25
4.	27	20	87.03	0.25
5.	9	3	22.20	0.22
6.	25	13	70.37	0.44
7.	18	6	44.40	0.30
8.	17	3	37.03	0.51
9.	19	13	59.25	0.22
10.	17	8	46.30	0.33
11.	19	6	46.30	0.48
12.	25	17	77.70	0.30
13.	27	15	77.70	0.44
14.	24	18	77.70	0.22
15.	26	14	74.07	0.44
16.	8	2	18.50*	0.22
17.	16	10	48.15	0.22
18.	19	10	53.70	0.33
19.	27	14	75.92	0.48
20.	19	12	57.40	0.26
21.	23	8	57.40	0.55
22.	25	14	72.20	0.40
23.	21	11	59.25	0.37

(Contd...)

Item No.	High	Low	D.V.	D.P.
24.	26	12	70.37	0.52
25.	22	9	57.40	0.48
26.	18	11	53.70	0.26
27.	20	8	51.85	0.44
28.	24	18	77.70	0.22
29.	26	14	74.07	0.44
30.	25	13	70.30	0.44
31.	27	22	90.70*	0.18*
32.	25	15	74.07	0.37
33.	25	13	70.37	0.44
34.	16	14	55.50	0.07*
35.	24	17	75.95	0.26
36.	25	9	62.96	0.59
37.	20	13	61.10	0.26
38.	24	14	70.37	0.37
39.	22	14	66.60	0.30
40.	27	19	85.18	0.29

* **Items deleted for the study.**

Item Selection

Four items were deleted for the final test as one item was very easy and the remaining three items could not discriminate high achievers from low achievers (as per the suggestions given by Noll et al., 1965). Overall thirty-six items carrying one mark each were included in the study.

Final Form of the Science Process Skills Test

The science process skills test consisted of thirty-six multiple choice type items. Total number of items in each process skill is displayed in the table given below:

Table 3.12: Number of items in each process skill

Sl. No.	Process skill	Item no. referring to the skill	Total no. of items
1.	Observating	1,3,8,11,26	5
2.	Hypothesizing	4,7,9,24,29,35	6
3.	Reasoning	2,14,17,22,32,34	6
4.	Predicting	10,16,20,21	4
5.	Interpretating	12,15,25,27,33,36	6
6.	Inferring	5,13,28,30,31	5
	Total		**36**

Approximately, equal number of test items was included in each category measuring the skills of observing, hypothesizing, reasoning, predicting, interpreting and inferring. The summated score was taken for analysis. Each question carried one mark. Students had to select one of the four alternatives in the test.

Reliability of the Test

The test retest correlation coefficient was (r = 0.95), which indicated the high reliability of the test.

(v) Scientific Attitude Scale

Scientific attitude as discussed earlier, is one of the most important outcomes of science education. It is a process that starts right from the very beginning in the immediate environment provided by the parents, friends, neighbourhood, school and society at a large. It refers to a particular approach a person makes for solving problems, for assessing ideas and information and for making decisions. This scale is used to measure the scientific attitude among the secondary school students. Even though many tools for measuring scientific attitude (Scientific attitude scale by Vardhini, 1983; Science attitude study by Dhani, 1989; Scientific attitude scale by Rao, 1997) were available, it was felt that there was a need to construct scientific attitude scale as the scientific attitude scales differ in their context, type of questions, purpose and so on.

Among Grinnell's twenty components of scientific attitude, the following seven were taken for the present study keeping the age and mental maturity of the students in mind.

(a) Curiosity

The following are the indicators found in a person who is curious.

1. Desire for understanding new situations that are not explained;
2. Find out the "whys" and "how's" of observed phenomenon;
3. Give emphasis on questioning approach of novel situations; and
4. Desire for completeness of knowledge.

(b) Rationality

A person who is rational shows:

1. Commitment to the value of rationality;
2. Tendency to test traditional beliefs;
3. Seeking of natural cause of events and identification of cause and effect relationship;
4. Acceptance of criticalness; and
5. Challenge of authority.

(c) Open-mindedness

An open-minded person demonstrates

1. Willingness to revise opinions and conclusions;
2. Desire for new things and ideas; and
3. Rejection of singular and original approach to people, things and ideas.

(d) Objectivity

The following are the indicators of objectivity:

1. Demonstration of the greater possible concern for observing and recognizing facts without any influence of personal pride, bias or ambition.
2. In interpreting results the individual does not allow any modifications according to present social, economic or political situations.

(e) Willingness to Suspend Judgment

A person with scientific attitude is:

1. Unwilling to draw inference before evidence is collected;
2. Unwilling to accept facts, things that are not supported by convincing proofs;
3. Avoids quick judgments and do not jump to conclusions.

(f) Free from Superstitions

The indicators of free from superstitions are:

1. Rejection of superstitious belief.
2. Acceptance of scientific facts and explanations.

(g) Perseverance

A person with perseverance shows:

1. Tendency to try till success is attained;
2. Acceptance of failures as steps for success; and
3. Believing in work as worship.

Among the different techniques available for the construction of attitude scale, the more popularly used techniques are: (a) the method of equal appearing intervals known as the 'Thurstone technique' and (b) the method of summated rating popularly known as 'Likert technique'. Likert technique and situational testing were used for the construction of scientific attitude scale. Likert scale was preferred in the present tool construction as there is a scope for the expression of intensity of an opinion through the scaled response besides being easy to construct. Likert items give the degree to which the subject shows his attitude favourable or unfavourable. The Likert type items give scope to test the cognitive and affective aspects of attitude and situational testing items assess the behavioural aspect of the attitude.

The situational test items were constructed by giving a situation followed by alternative behaviours and the students were asked to opt for a choice among the alternatives, which is more close to his choice. It is presumed that the pupil's choice of behaviour in that alternative would reflect his scientific attitude. Number of items including both likert type and situational testing were pooled from all the seven components of scientific attitude.

Item Pool

Likert type and situational testing type items were written based on the seven components of science attitude selected. The statements included both positive and negative items. The situations along with three possible solutions were provided to the students. The items were discussed with the experts and then changes were made wherever required. Two sections were made.

The Section I contained twenty-four situational testing items with three possible answers and scores corresponding to high (2), moderate (0) and low (1) scientific attitude. All the precautions were taken to avoid ambiguity among the options provided.

The Section II contains 24 Likert items that have to be answered on a five-point continuum ranging from strongly agree (SA), Agree (A), Undecided (UD), Disagree (D) to Strongly disagree (SD). The rating scale included twelve negative and twelve positive statements. Each positive item weighed a score of 2 for SA, 1 for A, 0 for UD, -1 for D and -2 for SD and a negative item -2 for SA, -1 for A, 0 for UD, 1 for D and 2 for SD.

The summative score of all the items from section 1 and section 2 provided the cumulative score of scientific attitude. In the Section I, items were jumbled up and were arranged in a random way. The following table shows the number of positive and negative items component wise in the Likert scale constructed.

Table 3.13: Number of positive and negative items in scientific attitude scale dimension-wise

Sl. No.	Components	No. of +ve items	No. of -ve items
1.	Objectivity	1	1
2.	Curiousity	1	2
3.	Open-mindedness	2	1
4.	Perseverance	2	1
5.	Rationality	3	1
6.	Free from superstitions	1	4
7.	Willingness to suspend judgement	2	1
	Total No. of items	**12**	**12**

(ii) Try Out and Item Analysis of the Scale

The scientific attitude scale thus prepared was subjected to try out. The test was administered to hundred eighth standard students of local schools of Mysore. Students were given specific directions to answer the test items and sufficient time was given to complete the test. The responses of the subjects were scored by allotting weightage to the items. The Item analysis of attitude scale was carried out to eliminate inconsistency of the items in the following method:

- The weighted score for each item, and also for each subject was summed up.
- On the basis of the total scores 27% of the high scores (High group) and 27% of the low scores (Low group) among the group were identified.
- The scored responses in terms of weighted scores for each item was tabulated separately for high and low groups and the mean score for each item was worked out.
- The Item analysis of scientific attitude scale was carried out by using 't' test for each of the forty-eight statements for the higher and lower groups.

- Thus the significance of difference between the means were calculated to find out the discriminating power of each item, as to how well each item can distinguish between individuals having different attitudes.
- Only those items that showed significant difference between high and low groups were selected for the final form of test.

The items, which have t value less than 1.18, were deleted from the final test.

Table 3.14: Item analysis of scientific attitude scale

Item No.	High groups		Low groups		't' Value
	Mean	S.D.	Mean	S.D.	
I1	2.93	0.27	2.70	0.61	1.65*
2	2.96	0.19	2.37	0.84	3.86
3	2.96	0.19	2.11	0.80	5.12
4	2.81	0.39	2.26	0.76	3.40
5	2.85	0.36	2.22	0.89	3.70
6	3.00	0.00	2.89	0.32	1.80
7	3.00	0.00	2.59	0.69	3.05
8	3.00	0.00	2.33	0.87	3.95
9	2.66	0.55	2.14	0.82	2.56
10	2.96	0.19	2.40	0.89	3.09
11	3.00	0.00	2.18	0.88	4.82
12	3.00	0.00	2.66	0.62	2.79
13	2.85	0.36	2.52	0.75	1.97
14	2.92	0.26	2.14	0.90	4.33
15	2.81	0.55	2.44	0.84	1.73*
16	2.81	0.39	2.48	0.70	2.21
17	3.00	0.00	2.48	0.70	3.85
18	2.40	0.69	1.89	0.84	2.21
19	3.00	0.00	2.56	0.75	3.07
20	2.74	0.52	1.96	0.89	3.85
21	2.92	0.26	2.22	0.84	4.44

(Contd...)

Item No.	High groups		Low groups		't' Value
	Mean	S.D.	Mean	S.D.	
22	2.85	0.36	2.29	0.72	3.60
23	3.00	0.00	2.26	0.81	4.73
24	2.56	0.51	2.04	0.76	3.36
II1	4.26	1.16	3.89	1.09	0.99*
2	3.07	1.41	3.11	1.42	-0.12*
3	4.93	0.38	4.48	0.85	2.59
4	4.37	0.74	3.40	1.59	3.07
5	4.11	1.08	2.74	1.06	4.83
6	4.44	0.93	2.81	1.46	4.88
7	4.11	1.18	3.51	0.93	2.12
8	4.29	0.95	3.51	1.36	2.29
9	4.66	0.55	3.52	1.19	5.46
10	4.44	0.80	3.33	1.49	3.66
11	4.67	0.48	4.03	0.80	3.38
12	4.55	0.69	3.51	0.93	6.00
13	3.92	1.03	3.14	1.19	3.01
14	4.22	1.08	2.92	1.32	3.67
15	4.30	1.06	3.48	1.31	2.13
16	4.77	0.57	3.59	1.47	3.55
17	4.26	0.94	2.92	1.38	4.56
18	4.55	0.64	3.74	1.12	3.18
19	4.55	0.84	2.89	1.42	5.43
20	4.66	0.62	3.67	1.20	3.99
21	4.66	0.48	3.44	1.18	4.84
22	3.77	1.33	2.67	1.20	3.16
23	4.81	0.48	3.44	1.31	4.75
24	4.89	0.42	3.63	1.41	4.13

* **Items deleted from the test.**

Final Form of the Test

Finally, four items i.e. 2 items each from section I and section II were deleted, as they failed to show significant difference between low and high groups. So the final form of the test included forty-four items i.e. twenty-two items in each section.

The following table shows the selected items under the seven categories of scientific attitude.

Table 3.15: Item numbers of components of scientific attitude

Sl. No.	Components of Scientific Attitude	Item numbers in the test		Total No. of items
		Section I	Section II	
1.	Objectivity	2,7,13,14,18	8,11,19	8
2.	Curiosity	3,11,22	9,17	5
3.	Open-mindedness	4,12,17	2,10,16	6
4.	Rationality	1,10,21	1,13,18,20	7
5.	Free from superstitions	5,8,16	6,12,15,22	7
6.	Willingness to suspend judgment	6,15,19	3,5,7	6
7.	Perseverance	9,20	4,14,21	5
	Total			44

Reliability of the Scale

The test retest correlation coefficient was found to be 0.66, which indicated the high reliability of the test.

(vi) Attitude Towards Science Scale

Modern science curricula emphasize the improvement of cognitive and affective domains in science. According to Gardener (1975) attitude towards science have predominantly affective orientation. Attitude towards science can be defined as a learned response evaluating ones feelings within the environment related to science learning. In the present study, to find out the effectiveness of constructivist approach on students attitude towards science, it was planned to develop a five point rating scale. Among the different techniques available for the construction of attitude scale, Likert's technique was adopted.

Attitude towards science scale was constructed based on the following dimensions:

- Using science materials to do science activities (investigative process)
- Perceived comfort or discomfort related to classroom science
- Learning science content
- Reading or talking about science related topics
- Viewing science programs on films or T.V.

The procedure followed for the construction of likert type attitude scale is described below:

Item Pooling

The Investigator first listed all the possible statements including both favourable and unfavourable statements in each dimension. These items were discussed with the experts in the field at different intervals to determine the relevance of items to be included in each category in order to avoid replication. Efforts were made to improve the language and to remove ambiguity and to make them comprehendible to the learners. The items collected were thoroughly screened and edited. Thus a total of fifty items on a five-point scale were included in the preliminary form of attitude scale.

Each item therefore contained five alternative responses such as strongly agree (SA), Agree (A), Undecided (UD), Disagree (D) and Strongly disagree (SD). The scoring based on a five-point likert type scale designed for positive item weighed a score of 5 for SA, 4 for A, 3 for UD, 2 for D and 1 for SD and for a negative item 1 for SA, 2 for A, 3 for UD, 4 for D and 5 for SD. The summative score of all the items provided total attitude towards science score.

Try Out and Item Analysis of the Scale

The attitude scale thus prepared was tried out on 100 students of eighth standard of local schools in Mysore. The item analysis was carried out in the similar way as in the case of scientific attitude scale. The result of the item analysis of attitude towards science scale is presented in the Table 3.16.

Table 3.16: Item analysis of attitude towards science scale

Item No.	High groups		Low groups		't' Value
	Mean	S.D.	Mean	S.D.	
1.	4.70	0.47	3.96	0.59	5.04
2.	4.78	0.58	4.11	1.12	2.94
3.	4.70	0.67	4.07	0.78	3.53
4.	4.70	0.67	4.11	0.85	3.05
5.	4.44	0.93	3.11	1.22	4.22
6.	4.74	0.81	4.52	0.58	1.10*
7.	4.07	1.04	3.07	1.04	3.31
8.	4.26	1.16	3.26	1.20	3.08
9.	4.67	0.83	3.85	1.17	2.99
10.	4.41	1.01	3.78	0.93	2.70
11.	4.74	0.45	4.15	1.03	3.31
12.	4.48	0.85	3.85	1.06	2.31
13.	4.59	0.89	3.81	0.56	3.99
14.	4.74	0.45	4.33	0.62	2.83
15.	4.63	0.84	3.96	0.90	3.34
16.	4.41	0.64	3.15	1.06	4.76
17.	4.59	0.75	3.37	0.74	6.05
18.	4.52	0.51	3.41	1.01	5.15
19.	4.41	0.80	4.04	0.94	1.55*
20.	4.59	0.64	3.93	0.87	3.22
21.	4.33	0.78	3.48	1.05	3.21
22.	4.52	0.64	3.48	1.12	4.09
23.	4.07	1.04	3.33	1.11	2.53
24.	4.52	0.58	3.52	0.98	4.54
25.	4.59	0.64	3.85	0.95	3.31
26.	4.74	0.86	4.33	0.68	2.09
27.	4.33	1.00	3.22	1.25	3.78
28.	4.37	1.11	3.04	1.16	4.72
29.	4.85	0.36	4.04	0.98	3.94
30.	4.44	0.80	3.48	1.01	3.80

(Contd...)

Item No.	High groups		Low groups		't' Value
	Mean	S.D.	Mean	S.D.	
31.	4.41	0.84	3.52	1.01	3.52
32.	3.96	0.90	2.67	1.27	4.52
33.	4.70	0.82	4.00	1.04	2.55
34.	4.59	0.50	3.33	1.07	5.47
35.	4.56	0.75	3.26	1.40	4.00
36.	4.78	0.42	4.07	0.62	5.05
37.	4.70	0.54	3.41	1.05	5.32
38.	4.70	0.67	3.89	0.80	3.94
39.	4.63	0.74	3.37	1.04	5.62
40.	4.41	0.80	3.48	0.98	3.79
41.	4.48	0.64	3.48	1.22	3.99
42.	4.30	0.78	2.63	1.15	7.36
43.	4.81	0.48	3.67	1.07	5.11
44.	4.67	0.62	3.81	0.88	4.02
45.	4.59	0.97	3.59	1.19	2.82
46.	4.30	0.72	2.85	1.23	6.00
47.	4.52	0.64	3.41	0.93	5.00
48.	4.00	1.18	3.37	0.88	2.26
49.	4.00	1.14	3.33	1.24	2.11
50.	4.96	0.19	3.96	1.02	5.19

* **Items deleted from the study.**

Final Form of the Test

Two items were deleted through item analysis from the attitude towards science scale, as they did not show significant difference between low and high attitude groups. The final form of attitude scale comprised of forty-eight statements including both positive and negative statements. Thus the maximum possible score on the whole attitude scale was 240 and minimum possible score was 48. A high score on the scale indicated a favourable attitude while a low score show an unfavourable attitude towards science.

Reliability of the Scale

The test-retest reliability coefficient of the attitude towards science scale was found to be high and positive. The r-value obtained was 0.65, which made the tool highly reliable. The reliability coefficients of all the tools constructed are tabulated below:

Table 3.17: Test retest reliability coefficients of the tests constructed

Sl. No.	Name of the test constructed	Test-retest reliability
1.	Achievement test in science	0.90
2.	Perception of nature of science test	0.70
3.	Science process skills test	0.95
4.	Scientific attitude scale	0.66
5.	Attitude towards science scale	0.65

(vii) Reaction Scale

A reaction scale was constructed in order to know the reactions of pupils towards constructivist approach adopted in teaching science. The reaction scale consisted of four main components namely

- The method used
- The classroom atmosphere
- The role of teacher
- The evaluation techniques used

With regard to each component, few sentences were provided that would help the students recall the experimentation period. The reaction scale included both objective and open-ended questions. The objective type items were framed in the question form, which could be answered on a three point scale i.e.

Yes/Sometimes/No.

For example: Was there any scope for you to discuss with one another in the class?

Yes/Sometimes/No

The students were supposed to tick one among the three options provided. The items were arranged component wise as different sections with a small introduction. Descriptive questions were asked after the objective questions. They were included to add up to the qualitative information to the study. The questions were mainly framed on the instructional skills, classroom environment, relationship between the teacher and the students and among the students, daily assignments given, and evaluation techniques used.

(viii) Semi-structured Interview

Interview was taken to elicit the views of students on treatment given to them. General interview guide approach was used for conducting the interview. This approach essentially involves having an outline of topics to be covered during an interview; however, the order in which the topics are addressed is not set. The questions are not formulated beforehand. Interview guide focused the data collection in four topics or areas namely:

1. Teaching using constructivist approach
2. Classroom climate
3. Role of teacher and
4. Evaluation techniques.

Each student was given an opportunity to give reply to the questions in the same categories. The time limit for interview ranged from 20-25 minutes.

Phase III-Implementation phase

The present study was a quasi-experimental study involving a non-equivalent pre-test and posttest design. In this design the effects of the treatments were judged by the difference between the pretest and post-test scores. This is compared with the control group where alternative strategy is made use of by regular science teacher.

This phase was carried out in three stages:

(i) Administration of the pretests

(ii) Treatment

(iii) Administration of the post-tests

Before the pretesting stage, permission was obtained from the concerned principals and subject teachers of the two schools. The time schedule for administering of pretests was made.

Administration of Pre-Tests

The final form of the tests arrived at after the try out was administered to the students of both the experimental and control groups as a pretest i.e. before treatment. The students were made comfortable and then the directions were given to them regarding answering the test. The students of both the experimental and control groups were simultaneously pretested on Ravens progressive matrices, achievement in science, perception of nature of science test, science process skills in science, scientific attitude, and attitude towards science one by one. One test was given each day for both the groups to avoid fatigue.

Implementation of Experiment

The instructional materials developed were implemented to the experimental group for a period of four months. On parlance with this, the science teacher of control group was consulted regarding the duration i.e. number of periods required for teaching the selected lessons, mode of teaching and assessment that she would follow in that group.

The investigator has systematically taught seven lessons using Personal or psychological constructivist approach to the students of experimental group, preceeded by systematically planned and formatted daily lessons based on constructivist principles. The researcher maintained a diary where the daily observations of classroom interactions were recorded. The classes were taken in the regular science periods of the schools. Some times the co-curricular activity periods were made use of for conducting laboratory experiments (150 periods).

In the control group, regular science teacher taught the students and covered the selected units approximately in the same number of periods. The science teacher of control group was known as an effective teacher in the school. The experimenter bias was avoided by involving the regular science teacher in teaching the control group students. The researcher observed the regular science teacher's classes in the control group during which the following observations were made.

- The lessons were not planned regularly by the teacher.
- The teacher explained the concepts with certain intermittent activities demonstrated.
- Scope was not provided to pupils to do activities on their own.
- Evaluation was not continuous and performance based.
- The end product of learning was given more importance rather than the 'process' or the 'procedure of learning'.

In the experimental group, the investigator created such an environment in the classroom that the students were able to construct the knowledge related to the given concepts and themes by doing various activities in which already known experiences and knowledge played a significant role. The investigator got continuous feedback from the experimental group students and their regular teachers. The lessons were audio recorded which added up to the feedback. The investigator made use of constructivist principles given by Brooks and Brooks (1995) in the class are as follows:

- Posing problems of emerging relevance to students.
- Structuring learning around primary concepts.
- Seeking and valuing students' point of view.
- Adapting curriculum to address students' suppositions.
- Assessing student learning in the context of teaching.

The investigator had also made use of ideas of Yager (1991) while implementing a constructivist format, which is as follows:

- Seek and use students' questions and ideas to guide lessons and whole instructional units.
- Accept and encourage student's initiation of ideas.

- Promote student leadership, collaboration, location of information and taking actions as a result of the learning process.
- Use student thinking, experiences and interests to drive lessons.
- Encourage the use of alternative sources for information both from written materials and experts.
- Encourage students to suggest causes for events and situations and encourage them to predict consequences.
- Seek student ideas before presenting teacher ideas or before studying ideas from textbooks or other resources.
- Encourage students to challenge each other's conceptualizations and ideas.
- Give adequate time for reflection and analysis; respect and use all ideas that students generate.
- Encourage self-analysis, collection of real evidence to support ideas and reformulation of ideas in light of new knowledge.
- Use local resources as original sources of information that can be used in problem resolution.
- Involve students in seeking information that can be applied in solving real-life problems.
- Extend learning beyond class period, classroom and the school.
- Focus the impact of science on each individual student.

Both individual and group work were given to the students. Various methods were used including role playing, field work, film watching, experimentation, group discussions, reflective thinking, hands on assessments, concept attainment games, conducting small class exhibition. Daily assignments in the form of worksheets were provided to the students. Lessons were planned three days before and were given to the guide and experts in that field to seek their comments. Based on their feedback, necessary modifications were made. Lessons were also audio recorded which also gave feed back time to time. The unit test was given as soon as each lesson was completed apart from daily assignments.

The audio-recorded lessons were transcribed and a few of them are given below:

Example 2

Concepts to be Attained

Transpiration, functions of leaves, types of leaves—simple and compound leaves.

Objectives to be Attained

Students are expected to understand the reason behind the variety of leaves found in the surroundings and various functions of leaves other than photosynthesis.

Strategy Used

Field trip to a garden and a greenhouse.

Process Skills to be Developed

Observing, predicting, hypothesizing, inferring, generalizing, drawing.

Attitudes to be Developed

Appreciation of the variety of leaves found, curiosity, willingness to suspend judgment, cooperation, and reverence for life.

Situation Provided

The students were intimated about the field trip on the previous day. The objective behind the field trip was also explained before the field trip. Instructions were given to the pupils regarding what they were supposed to carry, look for, and collect during the trip. They were asked to collect different types of leaves. The students were given utmost freedom to explore things.

Stage of Exploration

The students observed the leaves around them, discussed with each other about the color, size and texture of leaves collected.

After collection of the leaves they were asked to stick them on herbarium sheets. Some of the photographs taken during the field trip are given in the page nos.167, 168, 169. As soon as they returned, the teacher along with the students extended and deepens the experiences of the students.

On the next day, a group discussion was held on what pupils did on the previous day. The class participated in the discussion. Each one of them expressed their observations.

St1: The leaves are of different sizes, colours, textures, and shapes.

St5: Yes, even I too found a variety of leaves. Some are green; some are brown, some are white in colour.

St9: Some are small; some are very big in size; some have very rough surface where as some are soft, etc.

Tr: Very good. All of you all have collected a variety of beautiful leaves. Could you tell me why do we have so many varieties of leaves around us?

Students discussed among themselves.

S2: I read somewhere that cactus plants live in desert areas.

S7: May be that is the reason that they have leaves full of water.

S9: Yes, in social studies text I read that in coniferous forests the trees are cone shaped. It may be because of the rainfall.

St6: That means the leaves differ in their characteristics based on the environment in which they live.

St12: Yes, they adapt themselves to the surroundings. Even animals do.

Stage of Explanation

Tr: Why do you think there are so many types of leaves?

St: In order to adapt and cope up with the surrounding environment.

Tr: What are the coping mechanisms in case of plants?

St2: Some plants have thick spiny leaves e.g.: cactus in order to avoid evaporation of water from the leaves.

St3: They are not leaves; they are thorns.

St6: Do you know what is the process of evaporation of water from leaves called ?

St7: Don't know

St2: May be evaporation from leaves.

St3: In coniferous forests the trees are cone shaped in order to avoid water logging on leaves.

St4: We play on inclined planes, in the same way the water flows down when it is sloped well

St9: Even the leaves store food and water in many plants. We use the stored food in leaves in the form of vegetables in our daily life.

St7: Yes. Spinach, lettuce, mint are leafy vegetables which store food in the leaves.

St10: Yesterday I had seen a pitcher plant in discovery channel. It catches the prey.

St9: In Pitcher plant, the leaf looks like a cup; one more leaf covers as soon as any insect approaches near the cup.

St10: It was an amazing scene.

St9: Do you know what are those plants called?

St2: Insectivorous plants, as they capture insects in their trap.

St4: Its really interesting, what happens to the insect after getting trapped by the pitcher?

St9: May be it eats the insect.

St5: I don't think so.

Tr: The pitcher plant has certain digestive enzymes, which help in absorption of food material.

St2: I had seen some leaves of aquatic plants that are thin, ribbon shaped, some are bulbous in nature.

St4: What may be the reason behind the shape of the leaves?

St8: May be to allow the water to pass through them.

St10: Yes. As they cannot stop the water current, the leaves are thin, tiny and they allow water pass from them.

St9: To avoid spoilage of leaves.

Tr: Very good. You have listed so many functions of leaves.

Teacher repeats the points and writes down on the black board.

Stage of Expansion

Teacher using the ideas of the students explained that in order to adjust and sustain the plants adapt themselves to the environmental conditions. Those adaptations include leaves structure, shape, thickness etc. The leaves are designed in a plant based on its requirements. The plants living in water, in order to prevent water logging their body is structured in different ways such as thin, slender, ribbon shaped, with wavy stem, tiny leaves, leaves with less number of stomata and so on. Whereas in the plants living in high temperature i.e. desert areas, the leaves are modified into thorns and spines, the stem is very thick, storing water and performing the function of leaves.The plants in normal conditions have number of stomata on both upper and lower surface of the leaves and have thick woody stem etc. The leaves are of many types, but mainly they are simple and compound leaves. Simple leaves are with only midrib, where as in the compound leaves the midrib is branched and forms leaflets.

Tr: Ok. Students, try to identify the types of leaves, which we use as food. List out their uses.

Stage of Evaluation

Teacher asked the students to collect the leaves of xerophytes, aquatic and mesophytic plants and explained the coping mechanisms among them with examples. The students were also asked to identify the leaves and write the function of leaf in each case.

Example 3

Concept to be Attained

Circuit, Electricity.

Objectives to be Attained

To understand and define a circuit.

Additional Concepts that are Important for Expansion

Open or closed circuit, series circuit, parallel circuit.

Strategy Used

Experimentation, Problem solving method.

Attitudes to be Developed

Curiosity, open-mindedness, perseverance, positive approach to failure, cooperation.

Process Skills to be Developed

Observing, experimenting, predicting, classifying, inferring.

Stage of Exploration

Teacher's instructions to students: "Using only the three pieces of equipment given to you, light the bulb. Once you are successful, find three other ways to light the bulb. You can use only the three pieces of equipment you have been given. Carefully draw a picture of each method you used to try to light the bulb. Label your drawings as 'will light' and 'will not light'. Be certain to show exactly where your wire is touching and how your bulb is positioned with the battery".The equipment given to the students were a piece of wire, a cell, and a bulb.

The students tried to glow the bulb by trial and error method. They observed the things, discussed with each other, experimented and finally solved the problem.

St2: Battery is the source of electric current, bulb is the object given and lastly the wire is the medium through which current flows.

St4: That means we have to connect the bulb to the battery with the help of wire given.

St5: That's right.

Students connect it properly and the bulb glows.

Stage of Explanation

The students have drawn the pictures in their notebook. The students are asked to trace the pathway with their fingers that electricity from the battery flows through, when the bulb lights and when it does not light. So this path is known as a circuit. Using the students' ideas and words, the teacher constructed an explanation that a circuit is a pathway that electricity follows from the power source to the bulb and back to the power source.

Teacher showed the place of contact with the bulb must be made in two specific places. The path must be complete from the battery, through the bulb, and back to the battery for the bulb to light. The teacher asked a question: In how many places must the metal touch the bulb for it to light? The answer was two: the side and bottom conductors of the bulb must be included in the circuit.

Stage of Expansion

The teacher challenged the students to light more than one bulb, combine batteries for more power and add equipment such as a bulb holder, switch and more wires.

Students collect all the materials required, discuss with each other and draw the circuit diagrams.

St8: See, I think this way the bulb will glow. (It did not glow)

St9: Oh! here one bulb is unscrewed, may be that's why other bulbs are not glowing.

St4: Ya, the circuit is not complete, the power does not flow properly when all of them are not connected properly.

(they try again keeping all the bulbs screwed properly)

St9: Yahooooooo. I got it. The bulbs are glowing.

Teacher asked the student how did he do it?

The student showed and explained that he connected one bulb after the other continuously to the both ends of the battery.

Tr: What do you call this circuit?

St: No

Tr: It is called a series circuit as they are arranged in series i.e. one after the other.

St6: Madam, I too got it. But I had connected in a different way.

Tr: How did you do it?

St6: I had connected all the bulbs individually to the dry cell. One more interesting thing is even though if one bulb is unscrewed all the others remain glowing.

St9: That's great.

St9: May be this circuit is called parallel circuit as they are arranged parallel with each other.

Teacher asks the students to list the appliances used by electricity.

Students list the appliances like refrigerator, television, iron box, grinder, fans, bulbs etc. They appreciate the vast use of electricity in our daily life.

Tr: Students, I think all of you know who invented electric bulb. Do you know how many times Thomas Edison experimented before he successfully found a suitable material as a filament? Thousands of times he experimented with various materials and at last he succeeded with tungsten filament. Can you imagine the world without electricity? (perception of nature of science)

Students: Oh no, unimaginable, terrific.

St5: Its really great of science and technology that is improving day by day, which is making our lives comfortable. (Appreciation)

Stage of Evaluation

The students are given prediction sheets containing different circuit diagrams wherein they were asked to identify circuits as complete or incomplete by marking them the bulb as glowing or not glowing.

The students answered and discussed with the teacher about the circuits and got their doubts clarified regarding them.

The teacher asked the students to use the idea of a circuit to make a flash light out of the materials—cardboard tube, wire, two dry cells, flash light bulb, paperclip, bottle cap and tape at home.

The teacher gave a hand out in which they were asked to draw circuits for lighting for a house, as a home assignment.

The following are the photographs taken during the experimental treatment given.

Administration of Posttests

After the completion of the treatment both the experimental and control group were post tested on achievement in science, perception of nature of science test, science process skills test, scientific attitude and attitude towards science. Apart from the above tests the students of experimental group were given a reaction scale to give their reactions about the method used, the teacher, the classroom environment and the evaluation techniques used. Interviews were conducted to the students of experimental group to add the qualitative information in the study.

Statistical Techniques Used

The pretest, post test answer sheets obtained from the students of both experimental and control groups were scored as per the guidelines and scoring keys of each test. SPSS (10.0 version) was made use of for the statistical analysis of data. The following statistical techniques were used to analyse the collected data.

(i) Student 't' Test

't' test was used to know the significance of difference between pretest and posttest of various levels of objectives in an achievement test, dimensions of science process skills and scientific attitude.

(ii) Pearson's Product Moment Correlation

This technique was used to find out the correlation among achievement in science, perception of nature of science, science process skills, scientific attitude and attitude towards science.

(iii) Analysis of Covariance Test

As the design of the study demanded controlling the initial differences between experimental and control groups, analysis of covariance was employed. Univariate procedure provides regression analysis and analysis of variance for one dependent variable by one or more factors. It not only gives the effects of other variables on the mean scores of the various groupings of the dependent variable, but also the interactions between factors and as well as the individual factors. In addition, the effects of covariates and covariate interactions with factors are included.

4

Analysis and Interpretation of Data

Introduction

The present chapter focuses on the analysis of data pertaining to the effect of constructivism on students and interpretation of the results under six sections which are as follows:

- Section I deals with the analysis of the data related to the effectiveness of constructivist approach on achievement in science.
- Section II deals with the analysis of data pertaining to the effectiveness of constructivist approach on perception of nature of science.
- Section III deals with analysis of data pertaining to the effectiveness of constructivist approach on science process skills.
- Section IV deals with analysis of data related to the effectiveness of constructivist approach on scientific attitude.
- Section V deals with analysis of data related to the effectiveness of constructivist approach on attitude towards science.
- Section VI and VII deal with the correlation analysis and qualitative analysis of the data based on researcher's file, reaction scale and interviews conducted.

The experimental design chosen had no control over the pretest differences between control and experimental groups. Thus to control the initial differences, analysis of covariance test was employed. Both the pretest scores and intelligence were taken as covariates. In each section directional hypotheses were formulated and attempts have been made to verify those hypotheses using statistical techniques. All the data were processed and analysed using SPSS for windows (version 10.0).

SECTION I

Effectiveness of Constructivist Approach on Achievement in Science

In pursuance of the second objective, to study the effect of constructivist approach on the achievement of students in science, the following hypotheses were formulated:

H1: The constructivist approach does have a positive effect on the achievement of students in science.

H2: There will be a differential gain in the attainment of levels of objectives by constructivist approach over conventional method.

H3: There is a difference in achievement in science between girls and boys as an effect of constructivist approach.

H4: There is an interaction between 'gender' and 'groups' with reference to achievement in science.

To test the above hypotheses, analysis of covariance test was employed except for hypothesis 2. The results of analysis of covariance test for testing the above hypotheses are summarized in the following tables:

Table 4.1: Mean scores of achievement test of girls and boys of experimental and control groups

Group	Gender	N	Mean scores		Change
			Pre test	Post test	
Experimental	Girls	15	18.30	42.30	+24.00
	Boys	21	19.42	37.92	+18.50
	Total	36	18.95	39.75	+20.80
Control	Girls	15	17.50	22.20	+4.70
	Boys	17	21.05	27.47	+6.42
	Total	32	19.39	25.00	+5.61

Table 4.2: Results of analysis of covariance: Tests of between-subjects effects with respect to achievement in science

Dependent variable: Post achievement in science

Source of variation	Sum of squares	df	Mean square	F	Sig
Pre achievement	793.179	1	793.179	33.034	.000
Intelligence	91.108	1	91.108	3.791	.056
Group (A)	4157.408	1	4157.408	173.146	.000
Gender (B)	39.084	1	39.084	1.628	.207
Group*Gender (A*B)	258.767	1	258.767	10.777	.002
Error	1488.679	62	24.011		
Total	80391.00	68			
Corrected Total	7194.515	67			

Analysis of covariance revealed a significant difference in the pre-achievement scores ($F = 33.034$; $P<0.00$). After experimental treatment, a highly significant difference was observed ($F = 173.146$; $P<0.00$) between experimental and control groups, where mean score of the experimental group (39.75) is found to be significantly higher than the control group (25.00) as shown in the Table 4.1. The change of scores from pretest to posttest were 20.80 and 5.61 for experimental and control groups respectively. A large amount of change was observed in the experimental group, which can be attributed to effectiveness of experimental treatment (as shown in graph 4.11). Thus hypothesis 1 is proved to be true, i.e. the constructivist approach is found to be effective in improving the achievement of students in science. Therefore the hypothesis 1 proposed is accepted.

A majority of the students in the reaction scale expressed that the classroom environment had really helped them in their achievement. Thomas (1996) also supported the above findings. He found that constructivist learning environments had a positive impact on motivation and achievement among the students.

During the interview carried out to know the reactions of students belonging to the experimental group, one of the students said:

"This new method gave us an opportunity to understand and learn the concepts on our own. The various activities led us to better understanding of the concepts, sometimes by re-looking into the meaning of the concept and also helped in seeing relationship between concepts and even between the subjects. The assignments given and the tests conducted after the completion of every unit gave us a new direction wherein we had a variety of very interesting and challenging test items".

It is a known fact that better understandings always lead to better learning and then better achievement. Here it may be recalled that Kim (1994) and Banet (1997) had reported the significant positive effect of constructivist approach on better understanding and in turn better achievement among the students.

To verify the hypothesis 2, objective wise analysis was done. Paired sample 't' test was employed and the results are as follows:

Objective Wise Analysis of Data

It was found that the students of experimental group achieved better than that of the control group students. In the achievement test constructed (as discussed in Chapter III) the levels of objectives included are knowledge, understanding, application and skill.

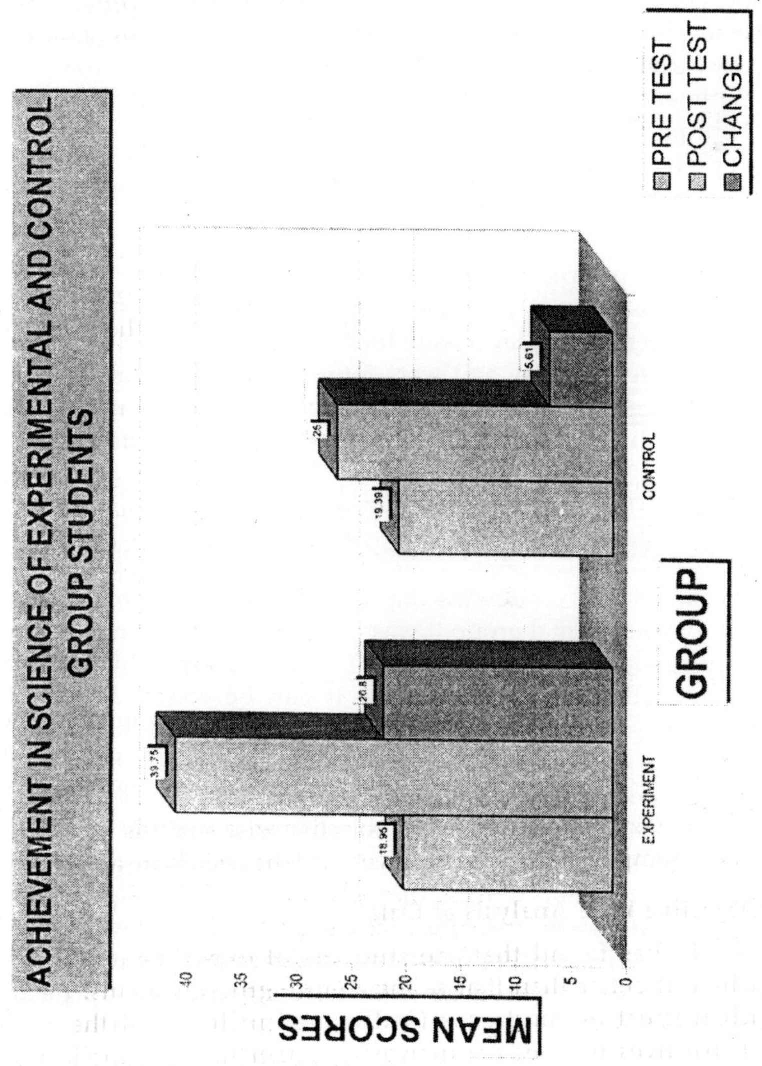
ACHIEVEMENT IN SCIENCE OF EXPERIMENTAL AND CONTROL GROUP STUDENTS
MEAN SCORES
0
5
10
15
20
25
30
35
40
18.95
39.75
20.8
19.39
25
5.61
EXPERIMENT
CONTROL
GROUP
PRE TEST
POST TEST
CHANGE

It is evident from the following table that in experimental group even though there is a significant difference between pretest and posttest mean scores in all the levels of objectives, the mean scores of understanding and application level were found to be greater than that of the other levels. Pretest and posttest mean scores and standard deviations of understanding level of experimental group were found to be 12.72 & 3.58, and 25.24 & 5.24 respectively, whereas 2.54 & 1.40, and 5.8 & 2.14 respectively for application level. As this method involved participatory mode of learning, it helped in improving the understanding and application level among the students.

It may be noted from the above Table 4.3 that the 't' values for the pretest and posttest of knowledge, understanding, application and skill level were found to be 8.135, 18.214, 10.959 and 9.659 respectively and were found to be significant at 0.01 level. Among the four levels of objectives, the 't' values of understanding and application level were predominantly high.

In the case of control group it is evident that mean difference was found to be higher in the case of understanding and application level with the 't' values of 5.690 and 2.656 respectively.

In both the groups the improvement was seen, but in the case of experimental group it was higher when compared to the control group (as evident from their 't' values). Thus the hypothesis 2 formulated is retained. Thus it can be concluded that constructivist approach is effective in fostering understanding and application skills among the students. The reason may be due to the additional strategies employed such as freedom given to the students for exploring, the class room atmosphere, the methods used like concept mapping, experimentation, role plays, classroom discussions, group works, film shows and field trips while teaching. Moreover, the constructivist principles followed, like encouraging the student questions, student initiation and more flexibility helped the students in the fostering understanding and application skills.

Between sexes, a non-significant difference was observed ($F = 1.628$; $P<0.207$). Thus the hypothesis 3 is rejected.

Table 4.3: Objective wise analysis of the achievement test scores

Objective	Stage	Expt.		Contl.		't' value		Sig.	
		Mean	S.D	Mean	S.D	Expt.	Cont.	Expt.	Cont.
Knowledge	Pretest	2.79	1.30	3.01	2.14	8.135	3.733	.000	.001
	Post test	6.22	2.29	3.96	1.45				
Understanding	Pretest	12.72	3.58	13.90	3.19	18.214	5.690	.000	.000
	Post test	25.24	5.24	17.12	4.49				
Application	Pretest	2.54	1.40	1.87	1.26	10.959	2.656	.000	.012
	Post test	5.82	2.14	2.96	2.09				
Skill	Pretest	0.89	0.66	0.59	0.48	9.212	2.438	.000	.021

It was also observed from the Table 4.2, that group and gender interaction also revealed a significant difference (F = 10.777; P<0.002). Hence the hypothesis 4 is accepted. Girls performed better than boys in experimental group. Where as in control group it is viceversa. In other words, girls (24.00) belonging to experimental group gained more when compared to other groups. In contrast to these findings, Pooran (2000) found that there was no significant interaction effects obtained for method of instruction (Constructivist approach) by gender.

Apart from the above observations, the constructivist principles (as discussed in the earlier chapter) used by the researcher, daily assignments, handouts, exercises and unit tests conducted helped the students of experimental group in improving their achievement. Continuous monitoring and periodical testing also helped to some extent for the high achievement of the students of this group. Unit tests given were analysed further to find out the progressive improvement in science among the students.

Analysis of Unit Tests

The answer sheets for every unit test was scored with the help of scoring keys and marking scheme and were converted into percentages followed by grading as per the following norms:

Table 4.4: Norms for the constructed unit tests

Percentage	Grade	Interpretation
0-20	1	Poor
21-40	2	Below average
41-60	3	Average
61-80	4	Good
81-100	5	Very good

The analysis of the unit tests was done to find out the progressive improvement in science among the students. It is clear from the table below that there were four students who showed poor performance in the first test and three students performed well.

Table 4.5: Frequency distribution of the scores of Unit tests

Units Grades	T-1		T-2		T-3		T-4		T-5		T-6		T-7	
	f	%	f	%	f	%	f	%	f	%	f	%	F	%
Poor	4	11.1	2	5.6	3	8.3	-	-	-	-	-	-	-	-
Below average	8	22.2	6	16.7	4	11.1	2	5.6	3	8.3	1	2.8	-	-
Average	21	58.3	21	58.3	14	38.9	14	38.9	5	13.9	2	5.6	4	11.1
Good	3	8.3	6	16.7	8	22.2	13	36.1	19	52.8	18	50	17	47.2
Very good	-	-	1	2.8	7	19.4	7	19.4	9	25	15	41.7	15	41.7

T-1: Metals and non metals

T-2: Magnetism

T-3: Electricity

T-4: Pressure

T-5: Conservation of natural resources

T-6: Organic evolution

T-7: How leaves are designed?

There were twenty-one average achievers in the first test. But there were no students of grade I found in the test 4 showing an improvement. Interestingly, in the first test there were eight below average students but gradually test after test the number reduced to zero. It was observed that there were no students coming under grade five in the first test, but gradually their number got raised from one to seven and then gradually to fifteen. Thus by the end of last test it was found that there were 4 average, 17good and 15 very good students. This shows that periodical testing and continuous feedback helped the students in the improvement of their achievement in science. This is further confirmed by contingency coefficient testing (X^2 = 106.59, P<. 000).

Daily Assignments

The daily assignments were analyzed to see the improvement among the students of experimental group that included both individual and group work. It was found from the analysis of the data that the students achieved better in the group assignments (Mean= 71.92) rather than individual assignments (Mean = 61.67). So the assignments given and the tests conducted after completion of every unit had contributed to the higher achievement in science among the students of experimental group. The analysis of reactions given by the students also revealed that the daily assignments given helped them in learning better. Among the group and individual assignments given, a majority of the students i.e. 31(86%) enjoyed the group work and expressed that they learnt better in group work than that in the individual work. The unit tests were given as said earlier after completion of every unit. On average 75% of students felt that the test items were challenging while answering the test paper and even expressed that they enjoyed answering the items involving concept maps in the test.

From the above reactions it is clear that the assignments and continuous evaluation helped the students belonging to experimental group in improving science achievement.

Unit Wise Analysis of the Achievement Test Scores

As discussed earlier in the previous chapter, seven units were selected for the treatment, which included physics, chemistry and biology lessons. It was intended to find out in which lessons the students improved their understanding and application levels. So the researcher had taken the total sum and percentages of all the levels of objectives for each lesson.

It was found that the units like 'Electric current, Magnetism, and Pressure' had more scope for activities, experimentation and were very much related to their daily life. The students had improved in achievement in unit-'Electric current' from 36 to 84% and 21 to 52% in answering understanding and application level items. The application level had improved in the Unit 'Magnetism' among pupils from 40 to 81%. The understanding of concepts in one lesson helped in learning new concepts in the same and different lessons. For eg., in the lesson 'Metals and their properties', the students had learnt various characteristics of metals where in magnetic property was also one among them. This helped them in understanding when 'Magnetism' unit was dealt. It helped the students in classification of magnetic and non-magnetic substances and in turn in understanding and achieving better. Even the concepts in 'Magnetism' unit helped in understanding the concept of electromagnet and others in the unit 'Electricity'.

In the similar way, concept of adaptation was learnt in 'Organic evolution' unit and it is very much related to the unit 'How leaves are designed?' The concepts understood by the students in first lesson helped them in reasoning out the existence of variety of leaves. This is one of the reasons that was responsible for progressive improvement in the unit tests conducted after completion of every unit. One more important reason for their improvement is the variety of experiences they had during the treatment like participation in role-plays, presentations, classroom discussions etc. All the above observations led to better achievement among the students of experimental group than their counter parts.

SECTION II

Effectiveness of Constructivist Approach on Perception of Nature of Science

The present experimental study also aims to find out the effectiveness of constructivist approach on the perception of nature of science among the eighth standard students. The following hypotheses were formulated in pursuance of the objective no. 3.

H5: The constructivist approach does have a positive effect on the students' perception of nature of science.

H6: There is a difference in perception of nature of science between girls and boys as an effect of constructivist approach.

H7: There is an interaction between 'gender' and 'group' with reference to perception of nature of science.

As mentioned earlier, analysis of covariance was employed to control the initial differences among the experimental and control groups. The pretest scores of perception of nature of science test and intelligence scores were taken as covariates. The results of the analysis of covariance test are tabulated here under.

Table 4.6: Mean scores of perception of nature of science of girls and boys of experimental and control groups

Group	Gender	N	Mean scores		Change
			Pretest	Posttest	
Experimental	Girls	15	15.80	21.27	+5.47
	Boys	21	14.33	20.76	+6.43
	Total	36	14.94	20.97	+6.03
Control	Girls	15	13.67	16.67	+3.00
	Boys	17	14.94	15.94	+1.00
	Total	32	14.34	16.28	+1.94

Analysis of covariance revealed a significant difference in the pretest scores of perception of nature of science ($F = 38.712$; $P<0.00$). After the treatment, a highly significant difference was observed ($F = 44.894$; $P<0.00$) between the experimental group and control group, where the mean score of the experimental group (20.97) was found to be higher than the control group (16.28) as shown in the Table 4.6. The change of scores from pretest to post test in perception of nature of science test was 6.03 and 1.94 for experimental and control groups respectively (as shown in graph 4.2). The high positive change in the perceptions of the students belonging to experimental group can be attributed to the effectiveness of the constructivist approach. Thus the hypothesis 5 was retained. This finding is concomitant with the findings of Blunck and Yager (1990), who also evidenced that students in classes taught with a constructivist approach improved more in their understanding of the nature of science when compared to students in classes taught with a textbook oriented approach. Adams (1997) in his study found that the students taught by constructivist model were found to have perceived science as relevant and useful to every day experience and also appreciated the importance of empirical evidence.

Table 4.7: Results of analysis of covariance-Tests of between-subjects effects with respect to perception of nature of science

Dependent variable: Post perception of nature of science

Source of variation	**Sum of squares**	**df**	**Mean square**	**F**	**Sig**
Pre perception of nature of science	291.194	1	291.194	38.712	.000
Intelligence	62.975	1	62.975	8.372	.005
Group (A)	337.696	1	337.696	44.894	.000
Gender (B)	6.361	1	6.361	1.244	.269
Group*Gender (A*B)	12.199	1	12.199	1.622	.208
Error	466.372	62	7.522		
Total	25322.00	68			
Corrected Total	1378.235	67			

Between sexes, a non-significant difference was observed ($F = 1.244; P<0.269$). Hence the hypothesis 6 was rejected. Analysis of covariance also revealed a non-significant interaction between group and gender on perception of nature of science ($F = 1.622; P<0.208$). Hence the hypothesis 7 was rejected.

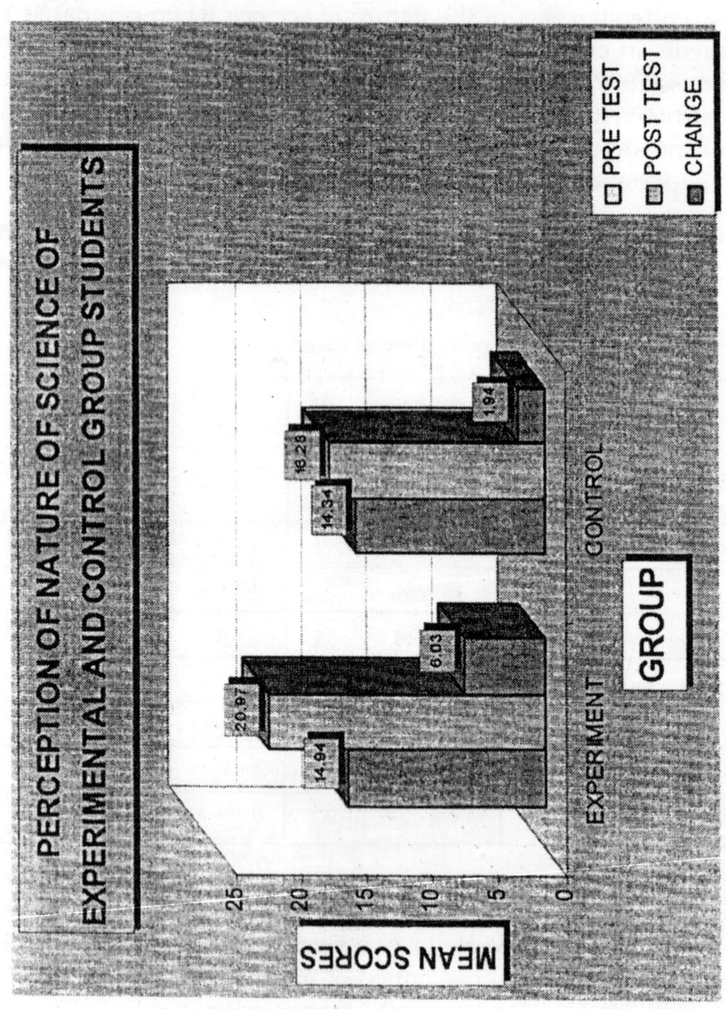
PERCEPTION OF NATURE OF SCIENCE OF EXPERIMENTAL AND CONTROL GROUP STUDENTS
MEAN SCORES
25
20
15
10
5
0
14.94
20.97
6.03
14.34
16.28
1.94
EXPERIMENT
CONTROL
GROUP
PRE TEST
POST TEST
CHANGE

Over all, constructivist approach was found to be an effective method in building up better perceptions of nature of science. Some of the students who underwent this innovation expressed:

"We had a variety of experiences like participating in role plays, conducting experiments in the lab, field trips. This had helped us in taking up the role of a scientist and in knowing what science is? What are its characteristics? How a scientific method differs from the unscientific ones? And so on. This method also gave us an opportunity to perform experiments by making use of scientific method. We had performed experiments repeatedly till we got correct answer. Especially, when we took the role of a scientist and acting accordingly, we could feel the dedication, serious ness and patience of a scientist. This experience helped us in not only knowing about the discoveries and inventions but also in knowing the characteristics of scientists and their method of study".

SECTION III

Effectiveness of Constructivist Approach on Science Process Skills

One of the main objectives of science education is to develop science process skills among the students. It was intended to find out the effectiveness of constructivist approach on the development of science process skills among the secondary level pupils. In pursuance of the above objective of the study, the following hypotheses were formulated.

H8: The constructivist approach does have a positive effect on the development of science process skills in students.

H9: There is difference in the development of selected science process skills as an effect of constructivist approach.

H10: There is a difference in development of science process skills between girls and boys as an effect of constructivist approach.

H11: There is an interaction between 'gender' and 'groups' with reference to development of science process skills.

Analysis of covariance was employed to test the above hypotheses except H9. The paired sample 't' test was employed to test H9. The results of analysis of covariance test for testing the above hypotheses are summarized in the following tables.

Table 4.8: Mean scores of science process skills of girls and boys of experimental and control groups

Group	Gender	N	Mean scores		Change
			Pre test	Post test	
Experimental	Girls	15	16.13	25.33	+9.20
	Boys	21	16.95	25.57	+8.62
	Total	36	16.61	25.47	+8.86
Control	Girls	15	17.66	18.93	+1.27
	Boys	17	19.88	20.23	+0.35
	Total	32	18.84	19.62	+0.78

Table 4.9: Results of analysis of covariance-tests of between-subjects effects with respect to science process skills

Dependent variable: Post science process skills

Source of variation	Sum of squares	df	Mean square	F	Sig
Pre science process skills	226.074	1	226.074	27.685	.000
Intelligence	36.043	1	36.043	4.414	.040
Group (A)	809.954	1	809.954	99.188	.000
Gender (B)	0.163	1	0.163	0.020	.888
Group*Gender (A*B)	0.976	1	0.976	0.120	.731
Error	506.283	62	8.166		
Total	365599.00	68			
Corrected Total	1795.691	67			

Analysis of covariance revealed a significant difference in the pre-process skills scores (F = 27.685; P<.000). After the experimental treatment, i.e. post-process skills test shown a significant difference between experimental and control group (F = 99.188; P<.000). From the table 4.8, the mean score of the experimental group (25.47) was found to be significantly higher than that of the mean score of the control group (19.62). The change of scores from pretest to post test were 8.86 and 0.78 for experimental and control group respectively (as shown in graph 4.3). This great change observed in the experimental group is attributed to the treatment given by the investigator. Hence the hypothesis 8 is retained.

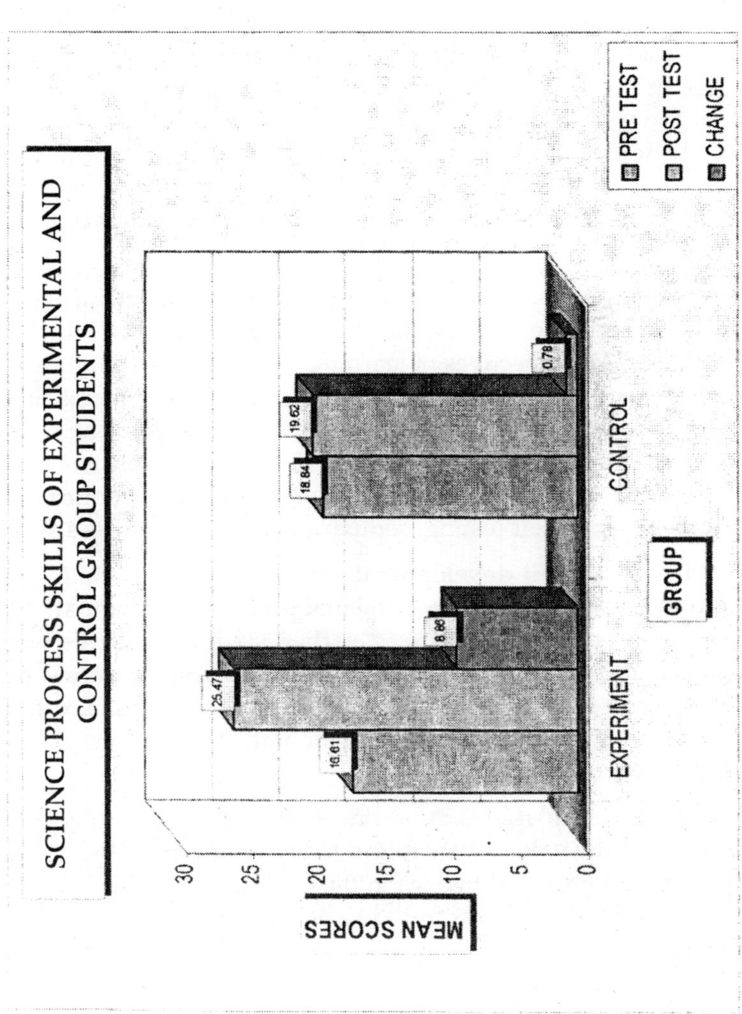
SCIENCE PROCESS SKILLS OF EXPERIMENTAL AND CONTROL GROUP STUDENTS
MEAN SCORES
0
5
10
15
20
25
30
16.61
25.47
8.86
18.84
19.62
0.78
EXPERIMENT
CONTROL
GROUP
PRE TEST
POST TEST
CHANGE

The results obtained may be attributed to the effect of constructivist approach implemented to the subjects of experimental group. The treatment had given them the opportunities to experiment and discover, in the process, developed the process skills of observation and other higher intellectual skills. For example, the students were involved in collecting the leaves during a field trip to a garden and a green house and were asked to make herbarium sheets on types of leaves. The students had to observe, differentiate the simple and compound leaves, see relationship between the habitat and the type of leaves and reason out why the leaves are structured in that way.

Thus the approach used, gave ample opportunities in developing science process skills among the students, which is one of the major objectives of learning science. Thus the students of experimental group were found to develop science process skills better than students of control group. The findings of the study conducted by Hyang-Lim (1995) also revealed that constructivist approach is effective in fostering observation, encouraging hypotheses and their testing, comparing and other process skills.

Thus, over all development of science process skills was found to be better in the experimental group when compared to the control group. As discussed earlier, six process skills were included in the present study. It was felt interesting to find out which process skills were developed better among the six, thus paired sample 't' test was employed for both the experimental and control groups.

The table 4.10 shows the 't' values of the science process skills, where in all the values were found to be significant in the case of experimental group. Where as in the control group the 't' values for reasoning (2.895), was found to be significant at .007 level of significance.

Table 4.10: 't' values for dimensions of science process skills

Process skills	Stage	Experiment		Control		't' value		Sig.	
		Mean	S.D	Mean	S.D	Expt.	Contl.	Expt.	Contl.
Observing	Pretest	2.61	1.02	2.53	0.91	5.351	1.438	.000	.161
	Posttest	3.36	0.86	2.78	1.07				
Inferring	Pretest	2.47	0.84	3.34	1.06	11.879	0.423	.000	.675
	Posttest	4.16	0.74	3.25	0.88				
Reasoning	Pretest	3.38	1.22	3.68	1.30	9.723	2.895	.000	.007
	Posttest	5.27	0.78	4.28	1.27				
Hypothesizing	Pretest	2.66	1.33	3.53	1.29	9.619	1.667	.000	.106
	Posttest	4.80	0.85	3.22	1.39				
Interpreting	Pretest	3.36	1.29	3.34	1.05	6.817	1.751	.000	.091
	Posttest	4.86	0.72	3.72	0.94				
Predicting	Pretest	2.11	0.95	2.34	0.98	4.781	0.150	.000	.882
	Posttest	3.00	0.92	2.38	1.10				

Among the six process skills the 't' value for inferring (11.879) was found to be greater in experimental group. The acquisition of science process skills were found in the order of inferring (11.879)> reasoning (9.723)> hypothesizing (9.619)> interpreting (6.817)> observing (5.351)> predicting (4.781). But in the control group the decreasing order of process skills was reasoning (2.895) < interpreting (1.751) < hypothesising (1.667) < observing(1.438) < inferring (0.423) < predicting (0.150). Thus it is very clear from the above observation that there is a significant difference in the development of various science process skills. Thus the hypothesis 9 is retained. It is well known that observing is the prerequisite skill for the development of the other skills. It is indicated from the table (4.10) that even though 't' value for observing was less, but improvement in the other process skills; hypothesizing, predicting and inferring subsumes the skill of observation which is basic to all other skills.

Between sexes, a non-significant difference was observed (F = 0.020; P<0.888) which indicated that constructivist approach was equally effective in fostering science process skills among girls and boys. Thus the hypothesis 10 is rejected.

The group and gender interaction was also revealed as non-significant (F =0.120; P<.731). In other words, there was no interaction between group and gender on the science process skills of students. Hence the hypothesis 11 is rejected.

SECTION IV

Effectiveness of Constructivist Approach Over Scientific Attitude

In pursuance of the fifth objective i.e. to study the effectiveness of constructivist approach on the scientific attitude of the students, the following hypotheses were formulated.

H12: The constructivist approach does have a positive effect on the scientific attitude of students.

H13: There is a difference in the development of selected scientific attitudes as an effect of constructivist approach.

H14: There is a difference in development of scientific attitude between girls and boys as an effect of constructivist approach.

H15: There is an interaction between 'gender' and 'groups' with reference to development of scientific attitude.

To test the above hypotheses, analysis of covariance test was employed except for the hypothesis 13. The results of analysis of covariance are summarized in the following tables.

Table 4.11: Mean scores of scientific attitude of girls and boys of experimental and control groups

Group	Gender	N	Mean scores		Change
			Pre test	Post test	
Experimental	Girls	15	119.20	126.00	+6.8
	Boys	21	114.80	124.33	+9.53
	Total	36	116.63	125.02	+8.39
Control	Girls	15	110.66	116.80	+6.14
	Boys	17	110.29	112.47	+2.18
	Total	32	110.46	114.50	+4.04

Table 4.12: Results of analysis of covariance:Tests of between-subjects effects with respect to scientific attitude

Dependent variable: Post scientific attitude

Source of variation	Sum of squares	df	Mean square	F	Sig
Pre scientific attitude	407.513	1	407.513	15.088	.000
Intelligence	676.082	1	676.082	25.032	.000
Group (A)	1275.238	1	1275.238	47.215	.000
Gender (B)	133.932	1	133.932	4.959	.030
Group*Gender (A*B)	51.248	1	51.248	1.897	.173
Error	1674.557	62	27.009		
Total	985723.00	68			
Corrected Total	5322.632	67			

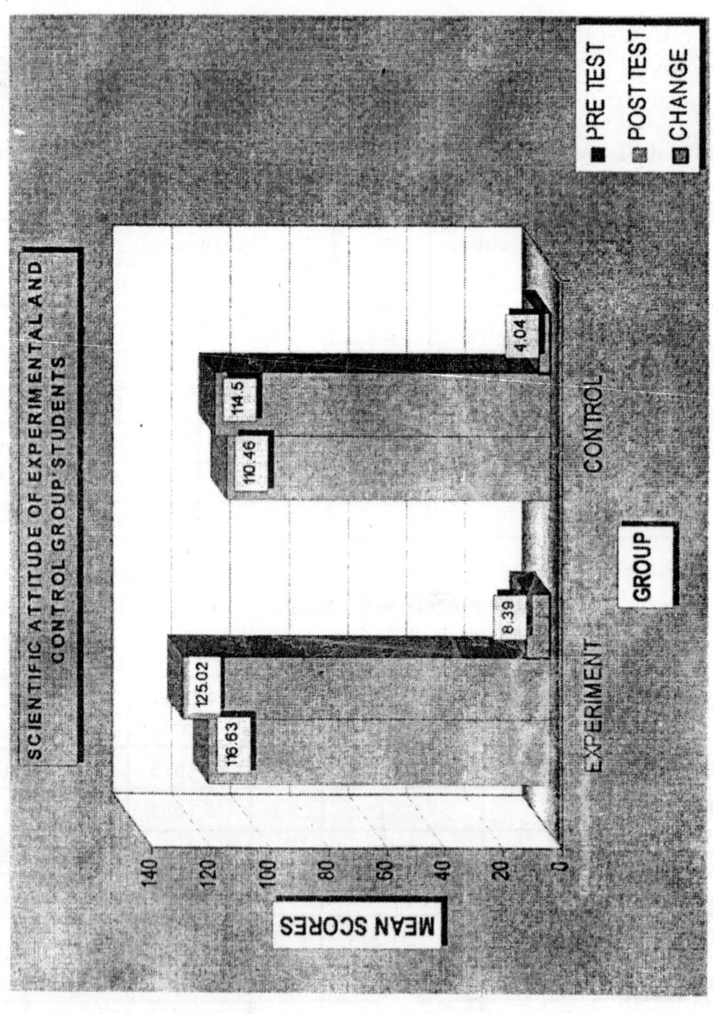
SCIENTIFIC ATTITUDE OF EXPERIMENTAL AND CONTROL GROUP STUDENTS
MEAN SCORES
140
120
100
80
60
40
20
0
116.63
125.02
8.39
110.46
114.5
4.04
EXPERIMENT
CONTROL
GROUP
PRE TEST
POST TEST
CHANGE

Analysis of covariance revealed a significant difference in the pre scientific attitude scores (F = 15.088; P<. 000). After the treatment given to the experimental group, a highly significant difference in scientific attitude was observed between experimental and control groups (F = 47.215; P<. 000) where mean score of the experimental group (125.02) was found significantly higher than that of the control group (114.50) as shown in Table 4.11. The change of mean scores from pretest to post test were 8.39 and 4.04 for experimental and control groups respectively(as shown in graph 4.4). In other words the students of experimental group improved better than that of control group on scientific attitude scale. Therefore the hypothesis 12 is accepted and retained.

In other words, the greater change in the scientific attitude of the students of experimental group can be attributed to the treatment given during the period of experimentation. The students were asked to discuss about the reasons behind some of the superstitious beliefs. They used to discuss and examine whether there is any scientific basis for those beliefs. For example when Magnetism lesson was taken up the teacher asked: "In which direction are we supposed to sleep?" Then a student said, "We should not sleep facing north direction, if we sleep we will get bad dreams". The students with the help of teacher tried to find out reasonable and scientific explanations behind such beliefs instead of taking them as a dogmatic belief. The students' inborn curiosity and rationality were fostered during the process.

The students were asked to bring an evidence for their answers doing some library work. The students on the next day came with various explanations and all of them were analyzed in the class and then the researcher used to conclude with a correct explanation.

In the similar way during laboratory periods, the students were allowed to experiment and were asked to find out the answers on their own. In the process of finding the answer, they had to try many sources and used to land up with number of answers for a single question. Ultimately the students have to find out the right answer. The students again used to check their answers by doing it again. With evidence in hands the students who went wrong used to accept their mistake. In this way they had developed an attitude of suspending judgments when evidence is found.

As stated earlier in the chapter III seven dimensions of scientific attitude were included in the present study namely objectivity, curiosity, open-mindedness, rationality, free from superstitions, willingness to suspend judgment and perseverance. To find out whether there is any difference in development of various dimensions of scientific attitude, as a result of constructivist approach, paired sample 't' test was employed.

From the table 4.13, it is clear that even though 't' values for all the seven dimensions were significant except for open-mindedness, the 't' value for free from superstitions (5.48) was found to be greater and significant even at .000 levels in the experimental group. Whereas in the control group the analysis revealed that the' t' values were significant only for rationality, free from superstitions, perseverance and objectivity.

The mean difference and in turn the 't' values were found in the following order in the experimental group: free from superstitions (t = 5.48) > curiousity (t = 5.06) > rationality (t = 4.21) > objectivity (t = 4.210) > perseverance (t = 3.83) > willingness to suspend judgement (t = 3.57) > open-mindedness (t = 0.916). Hence the hypothesis 13 is retained. Thus, the students of experimental group were found to have better scientific attitude after the treatment than their counter parts.

From the Table 4.12, it is also clear that there existed a significant difference in the scientific attitude of girls and boys (F = 4.959; P< .030). Hence hypothesis 13 is retained. Girls seemed to have scored better than boys on scientific attitude scale.

Group and gender interaction also revealed a non-significant difference (F = 1.89; P<0.173). Hence the hypothesis 15 is rejected.

SECTION V

Effectiveness of Constructivist Approach on Attitude Towards Science

The following hypotheses were formulated in pursuance of the objective 6 i.e. to find out the effectiveness of constructivist approach on attitude towards science among the eighth standard students.

Table 4.13: 't' values for dimensions of scientific attitude

Scientific attitudes	Stage	Experiment		Control		't' value		Sig.	
		Mean	S.D	Mean	S.D	Expt.	Contl.	Expt.	Contl.
Objectivity	Pretest	20.72	2.25	19.81	2.22	4.210	1.959	.000	.059
	Posttest	22.50	2.09	20.84	2.38				
Curiousity	Pretest	12.86	1.51	12.63	1.36	5.060	1.179	.000	.247
	Posttest	14.17	0.81	13.03	1.82				
Openmindedness	Pretest	16.81	1.28	15.78	1.68	0.916	1.325	.366	.195
	Posttest	17.03	1.00	16.16	1.67				
Rationality	Pretest	18.39	1.87	17.66	2.28	5.030	2.340	.000	.026
	Posttest	19.97	1.40	18.81	1.87				
Free from superstitions	Pretest	17.97	2.30	16.06	2.78	5.480	2.785	.000	.009
	Posttest	19.75	1.20	17.53	2.53				
Willingness to suspend judgement	Pretest	16.25	1.90	15.03	2.31	3.570	0.852	.001	.401
	Posttest	17.31	0.71	15.44	2.05				
Perseverance	Pretest	13.64	0.96	13.34	1.43	3.830	2.046	.000	.049
	Posttest	14.31	0.47	12.63	1.56				

H 16: The constructivist approach does have a positive effect on the students' attitude towards science.

H 17: There is a difference in attitude towards science between girls and boys as an effect of constructivist approach.

H 18: There is an interaction between 'gender' and 'groups' with reference to development of attitude towards science.

To test the above hypotheses, analysis of covariance was carried out. The results are summarized in the following tables.

Table 4.14: Mean scores of attitude towards science of girls and boys of experimental and control groups

Group	Gender	N	Mean scores		Change
			Pretest	Post test	
Experimental	Girls	15	201.00	215.80	+14.80
	Boys	21	196.57	215.57	+19.00
	Total	36	198.42	215.67	+17.25
Control	Girls	15	193.13	199.47	+6.34
	Boys	17	189.18	190.82	+1.64
	Total	32	191.03	194.88	+3.85

Table 4.15: Results of analysis of covariance: Tests of between-subjects effects with respect to attitude towards science

Dependent variable: Post attitude towards science

Source of variation	Sum of squares	df	Mean square	F	Sig
Pre attitude towards science	8018.284	1	8018.284	38.768	.000
Intelligence	124.718	1	124.718	0.603	.440
Group (A)	4291.177	1	4291.177	20.748	.000
Gender (B)	86.925	1	86.925	0.420	.519
Group*Gender (A*B)	303.448	1	303.448	1.467	.230
Error	12823.277	62	206.827		
Total	2911726.00	68			
Corrected Total	29373.059	67			

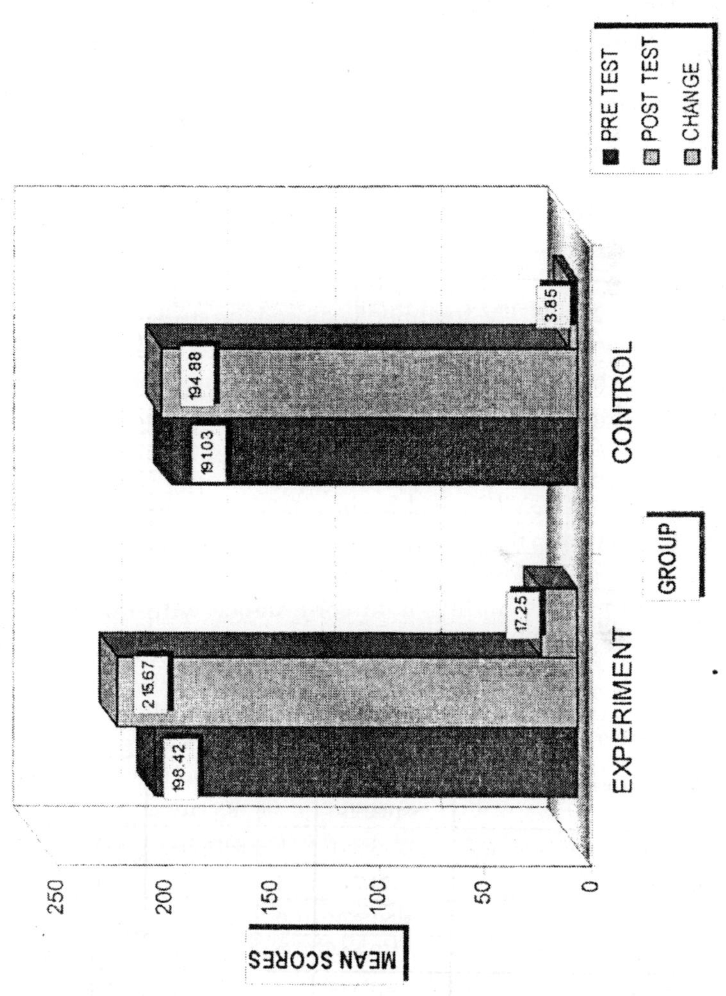
MEAN SCORES
250
200
150
100
50
0
198.42
215.67
17.25
191.03
194.88
3.85
EXPERIMENT
CONTROL
GROUP
PRE TEST
POST TEST
CHANGE

Analysis of covariance revealed a significant difference in the pre attitude towards science test scores (F = 38.768; P<.000). After the experimental treatment, between experimental and control groups, a highly significant difference was observed (F = 20.748; P<.000) where mean score of the experimental group (215.67) is found to be significantly higher than that of the control group (194.88) as shown in the Table 4.14. The change of scores from pre to post test were 17.25 and 3.85 for experimental and control groups respectively (as shown in graph 4.5). It means that the subjects exposed to constructivist approach were found to have improved positive attitude towards science than their counter parts. Hence the hypothesis H16 is accepted and retained.

The improved favourable attiude towards science is attributed to the effective treatment given to the students of experimental group. The treatment exposed the students to nature of science, scientific method, various methods to obtain scientific knowledge etc. The students learnt many things on their own through trial and error method. The students were taught through methods like experimentation, reflective questioning, film shows, participation in debates, role-plays, and field trips etc, helped the students in building a favourable attitude towards science. It may be concluded that in the present study the subjects of experimental group developed a positive attitude towards science than the control group. This finding is in congruence with the studies conducted by Blunck and Yager (1990), Yore (1997) and Pooran (2000) who found that students in classes taught with a constructivist approach develop more positive attitudes toward science when compared to students in classes taught with a textbook oriented approach. Therefore, it can be said that high positive attitude towards science is one of the attributes for the higher achievement in the students of experimental group.

Sherri (1995) also found in his investigation that the favourable attitude towards science led to high science achievement of students. He examined the effects of constructivist learning environment on attitude towards science compared to students enrolled in a traditional course. The constructivist course utilized cooperative grouping and learning with very little lecture method. Quantitatively, students said that they enjoyed science more if constructivist strategies, instructor interaction, hands on activities and applications to daily life were used. The experimental group subjects were found to have high positive attitudes than their counter parts.

Between sexes, a non-significant difference was observed (F = 0.420; P<.519). Thus the hypothesis 17 is rejected.

Also group and gender interaction revealed a non-significant difference (F = 1.467; P< .230), indicating that there is no significant interaction between group and gender in developing a favorable attitude towards science among the secondary level students.

Hence from the above discussions, it can be concluded that the constructivist approach was effective in fostering achievement in science, perception of nature of science, scientific attitude, science process skills and attitude towards science of VIII standard students.

In order to know which variable among achievement, perception of nature of science, science process skills, scientific attitude and attitude towards science is more influenced by the constructivist approach, the percentages for the change in the mean scores were found and are tabulated in the following table.

Table 4.16: Mean scores of all the variables of experiment group

Dependent variables	Mean scores		Change in mean scores	% of change
	Pretest	Post test		
Achievement in science	18.95	39.75	+20.80	34.66
Perception of nature of science	14.94	20.97	+6.03	20.10
Science process skills	16.61	25.47	+8.86	24.61
Scientific attitude	116.63	125.02	+8.39	9.53
Attitude towards science	198.42	215.67	+17.25	7.18

From the table 4.16 it is clear that among all the variables, there is enormous change in the scores from pretest to post test in the achievement in science of students belonging to experimental group (20.79). There is 34.65 percent raise in the achievement of students (as shown in graph 4.6). It is also evident that there is greater improvement in the science process skills from the pretest to post test (24.61) among the students. Hence from the above discussion it is clear that constructivist approach is effective in improving achievement, perception of nature of science, science process skills, scientific attitude and attitude towards science of eighth standard students.

SECTION VI

Correlational Analysis

It can be concluded that constructivist approach is effective in fostering achievement in science, perception of nature of science, science process skills, scientific attitude and attitude towards science of eighth standard students. To find out whether there is a relationship among the above variables, the following hypotheses were formulated:

H19: There is a positive relationship between students' perception of nature of science and their achievement in science.

H20: There is a positive relationship between students' science process skills and their achievement in science.

H21: There is a positive relationship between students' scientific attitude and their achievement in science.

H22: There is a positive relationship between students' attitude towards science and their achievement in science.

H23: There is a positive relationship between students' perception of nature of science and their science process skills.

H24: There is a positive relationship between students' perception of nature of science and their scientific attitude.

H25: There is a positive relationship between students' perception of nature of science and their attitude towards science.

H26: There is a positive relationship between students' science process skills and their scientific attitude.

H27: There is a positive relationship between students' science process skills and their attitude towards science.

H28: There is a positive relationship between students' scientific attitude and their attitude towards science.

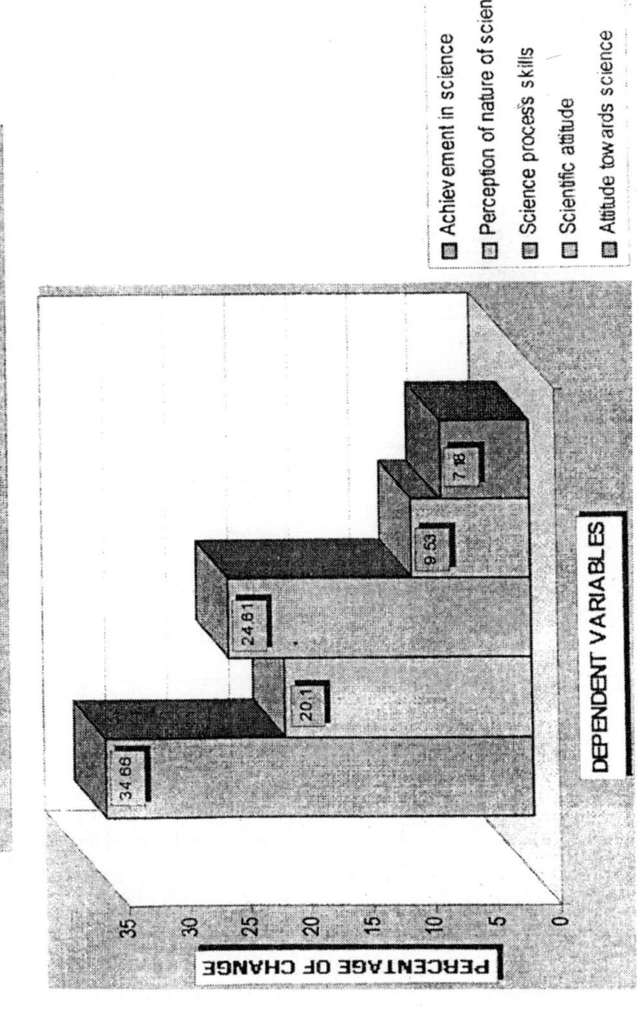
EFFECTIVENESS OF CONSTRUCTIVIST APPROACH ON DEPENDENT VARIABLES OF THE STUDY
PERCENTAGE OF CHANGE
35
30
25
20
15
10
5
0
34.68
20.1
24.61
9.53
DEPENDENT VARIABLES
Achievement in science
Perception of nature of science
Science process skills
Scientific attitude
Attitude towards science

To test the above hypotheses, pearson's product moment correlation was employed. The table below describes the relation of variables with each other and the hypotheses were verified based on the following results.

Table 4.17: Pearson's product moment correlation coefficients showing the relationship among the variables included in the study

Sl. No.	Variable 1	Variable 2	r	Sig.
1.	Perception of nature of science	Achievement in science	0.695	.000
2.	Perception of nature of science	Science process skills	0.598	.000
3.	Perception of nature of science	Scientific attitude	0.599	.000
4.	Perception of nature of science	Attitude towards science	0.424	.000
5.	Science process skills	Achievement in science	0.696	.000
6.	Science process skills	Scientific attitude	0.668	.000
7.	Science process skills	Attitude towards science	0.508	.000
8.	Scientific attitude	Achievement in science	0.649	.000
9.	Scientific attitude	Attitude towards science	0.628	.000
10.	Attitude towards science	Achievement in science	0.456	.000

The correlation matrix revealed that all the variables are positively related with each other. From the above table, it is evident that there exists a significant relationship between achievement in science and perception of nature of science as the correlation coefficient value obtained (0.695) was found to be significant at .000 levels. It is indicating a positive relationship between achievement and perception of nature of science. Hence the hypothesis 19 is retained. It may be interpreted that the better perception of nature of science will lead to better achievement in science as they are positively related to each other.

The Table 4.17 also indicated a positive correlation between science process skills and achievement in science. It is clear from the correlation coefficient value i.e. 0.696, that there is a high positive relation between science process skills and achievement in science. The students explore the environment by observing, measuring, hypothesizing, predicting, interpreting, inferring etc and in turn acquire knowledge. Thus it can be explained as, the greater the development of science process skills, greater will be the achievement in science. Thus the hypothesis 20 is accepted and retained.

By seeing the correlation coefficient value ($r = 0.649$; $P < .000$) for scientific attitude and achievement in science, it is evident that there exists positive relationship between them. Thus the hypothesis 21 is accepted and retained.

The Table 4.17 also indicated a significant positive relation between attitude towards science and achievement in science ($r = 0.456$; $P < .000$). Thus the hypothesis 22 is retained.

It is clear from the above table that perception of nature of science is positively correlated with science process skills ($r = 0.598$; $P < .000$), scientific attitude ($r = 0.599$; $P < .000$) and attitude towards science ($r = 0.424$; $P < .000$). Thus the hypothesis 23, 24 and 25 are accepted and retained.

The correlation coefficients also indicated that a significant positive relation exists between science process skills and scientific attitude($r = 0.668$; $P < .000$) and also attitude towards science($r = 0.508$; $P < .000$). Hence hypothesis 26 and 27 are accepted and retained.

It was also found that there is a positive relation between scientific attitude and attitude towards science. The correlation coefficient value obtained was 0.628 significant at 0.000 level. Thus the hypothesis 28 is accepted and retained.

Hence it was clear from the above observations that achievement in science, perception of nature of science, science process skills, scientific attitude and attitude towards science are positively related with each other.

SECTION VII

A Study of Students' Reactions About Constructivist Approach

Till now, the data collected was analyzed and interpreted quantitatively. It was felt essential to record qualitative information along with the quantitative data. Thus the observations recorded during the treatment by the researcher and the regular teachers, transcriptions of the audio recorded lessons, responses of the students on reaction scale, and the interviews conducted with the students were analysed qualitatively in this section. This information was collected to get a complete picture of what exactly happened in the class room and the reactions of the students towards new approach i.e. constructivist approach in teaching science. This section is dealt in the following headings:

Analysis of Students' Reactions

As discussed in the earlier chapter, the reaction scale consisted of four main components namely the method used; the classroom atmosphere; the role of teacher and the evaluation techniques used. The students of experiment group were given a reaction scale after the treatment and were asked to express their reactions about science teaching through the constructivist approach.

Students' Reactions on the Constructivist Method

For the question,

1. Which method of teaching do you like the most among the given two?

   (a) Teaching through regular method.

   (b) Teaching by the method used by the researcher.

Out of 36 students, thirty four (94.4%) of them answered (b). Only two students answered the regular teachers method, which showed that the majority of the students liked the new method.

- Thirty-two students even expressed that they have learnt the science content meaningfully.
- Thirty-five students opined that the researchers questions helped them in seeing relationship between the concepts learnt earlier and the present ones.

- 77.8% of the students were also involved in locating materials.
- Twenty-eight students (77.8%) found group work as interesting and useful. And 6 students felt individual work as interesting and the remaining felt the same in both conditions.
- It is interesting to note here that 28 students opined that apart from knowledge construction, this method also helped them in understanding each other in a better manner and helped in building self-confidence (32 students).

Overall, as a teaching method, constructivist approach was felt interesting and useful. The involvement from student side was more. It was child-centered approach where in the teacher's job is to facilitate and guide them by asking number of probing questions. The students were involved in many activities like concept mapping, role plays, group discussions, presentations which involved both individual and group works.

Apart from instruction, one important factor related in this context was classroom atmosphere.

Students' Reactions on Classroom Atmosphere

- Eighty-six percent of students expressed the class had democratic atmosphere where in they were given opportunity to talk, discuss, experiment and subject their ideas for verification.
- Thirty-four students expressed that they were very frank in giving responses and enjoyed lessons in researchers class.
- 94.4 per cent of students said that they were given freedom to ask questions.
- Thirty-four students also expressed that the method used had room for clarification of doubts and lot of scope was there to discuss with one another also with the teacher in the class.

- ❖ Twenty-nine students expressed that they were also given opportunity to conduct experiments in the class.
- ❖ One more interesting thing was that twenty-seven students expressed that they had taken initiative to plan and perform activities in the class.
- ❖ Even thirty students strongly felt that the classroom environment helped in learning better. It also gave opportunity in building good relationship with the teacher.

Over all, the classroom atmosphere was felt democratic, free for students to explore, examine, experiment and evaluate on their own which was the ultimate aim of science education. The teacher is an important element for the classroom atmosphere.

Students' Reactions on the Role of Teacher

- ❖ All the students felt that the teacher acted as one among them unlike a conventional teacher.
- ❖ The teacher was very friendly, gave lot of freedom to experiment in and out of the class.
- ❖ Thirty-two students expressed that the teacher gave chance to every one in the class to explain their views before she gets into the topic and that helped them in modifying their views.
- ❖ Twenty-eight students even told that their ideas were encouraged and accepted by the teacher and were also used in the class.
- ❖ Almost all students said that there is no need for repetition of the lessons taught by their regular teacher again.
- ❖ Twenty-nine students said that they were given opportunities to express their doubts and were clarified by the teacher.

Students' Reactions on Evaluation Techniques Used

After the completion of every unit, a test was conducted. The unit tests conducted included a variety of test items like fill in the blanks, match the following, classification type, multiple choice, short answer and essay type questions. All the test items were framed in such a way that they focus on the construction of knowledge rather than just testing the knowledge. The students were given ample opportunities to apply the principles learnt in solving the problems. More of understanding and application level items were included in the tests.

Various evaluation techniques such as worksheets, reflective questioning, description of concept maps, rating scales and so on were made use of for assessing the students' knowledge, understanding, application, skills, attitudes and so on. Evaluation was inbuilt in the constructivist method used while teaching the seven units of science. The reactions towards the evaluation techniques were as follows:

- Twenty-eight students i.e. 77% enjoyed answering the test items given in every unit test.
- Seventy-five percent of the students found the items challenging while answering the test.
- Thirty-one students i.e. 86% enjoyed answering the items involving concept maps in the test.

Interviews

Apart from the reaction scale, semistructured interviews were conducted to the students of experimental group as said earlier. Most of the highly intelligent students expressed that this method gave them an opportunity to perform challenging tasks and helped them in improving self-confidence. They even said that the test items were very interesting and challenging and gave more scope for self-expression. When asked about their researcher teacher, they expressed that the teacher was less involved in the classroom activities, very friendly, approachable i.e. like one among them unlike their regular teachers.

Some of them even expressed

"Previously we used to cram the answers and write in the tests but this new method of teaching and learning process, daily assignments including variety of exercises, various type of test items in unit tests helped us in improving in science achievement. Now I feel science as

very interesting subject, it is not just knowledge but it is a route to find knowledge and helps in finding solutions to problems. We were allowed to explore in the natural environment. We had participated in various activities like projects, experimentation, collection of various leaves in a field trip, watching films, played various games, played role plays and so on. Among them we liked the most role-plays. We took the role of scientists, we understood the nature of science and as well as scientists during role play."

Some of the below average students said

"I felt this method as very difficult, every time the teacher used to ask what do we know before and then the lesson used to be started, and then daily assignments were given, it was very difficult to us to answer them because the assignments many times were out of the text book, we went to library, we used to discuss with the teacher about the sources. Like this we were very busy through out the researchers class. Later around twenty days we could find this method not so difficult but really it helped me in learning better. Especially group activities gave a scope to discuss with each other, share the views and helped in improving ourselves. We started understanding each other. I feel in every subject we should have daily assignments. The teachers used to teach the concepts based on our ideas, this method gave scope to re look our ideas and correct them in time".

Daily Assignments

The daily assignments including individual and group work were given to the students. Thirty-one students expressed that the daily assignments given to them helped them in learning better. Among the group and individual assignments given, majority of the students i.e. 31(86%) enjoyed the group work and expressed that they learnt better in group work than that of the individual work.

The students were made to use sources other than their science textbook. They used to make use of their school library, gather information from their elders at home, even from Internet and so on to complete their assignments. First few days, number of assignments returned was very few. Later, all the students were very regular in submitting their assignments. Some of the students used to bring additional information to the class and the discussions were held based on that. Many of the students showed their enthusiasm in answering the daily assignments and project works given. Even the researcher got appreciation from the parents and other teachers in this regard. The students who never used to do any homework given have also submitted their work in time gradually.

Hence from the above discussion, it was clear that the classroom atmosphere, daily assignments, teaching method, various strategies and teaching techniques used during the treatment and evaluation techniques helped the students in the improvement in achievement in science, perception of nature of science, scientific attitude, science process skills and attitude towards science.

During the initial days of the treatment there was a lot of indiscipline among students. The researcher had to face the other teachers and so on. The students used to hesitate to question and even to answer. After few days the students got used to the method and started discussing with their friends and also with the teacher. They even took initiative in performing experiments in the class. It was also found difficult to arrange for group activities in the class, but later the students got adjusted to the class work. One of the regular teachers who had observed the class had commented that the students were giving multiple responses, some were disturbing the class and few were not at all involved in the classroom discussions in the initial stages. Keeping the feed back in mind the classes were dealt with all measures required in imparting self-discipline among the students.

Discussion

The aim of the research is to study the effectiveness of constructivist approach in learning science among secondary level students. This was carried out through a quasi-experimental design, where in the data was collected before and after the treatments. The data was analysed and the results indicate that a highly significant difference in achievement in science was observed ($F = 173.146$; $P<0.00$) between experimental and control groups, where mean score of the experimental group (39.75) is found to be significantly higher than the control group (25.00). The change of scores from pretest to posttest were 20.80 and 5.61 for experimental and control groups respectively.

Some of the empirical studies conducted by Thomas (1996); Kim (1994) and Banet (1997) also seemed to be in tune with this finding. They found that constructivist learning environments had a positive impact on motivation and achievement among the students. They also reported that there is a significant positive effect of constructivist approach on better understanding and in turn better achievement among the students.

The students were given daily worksheets and activity sheets where in they used to record their observations and results. The activities were further reinforced by expansion, discussion and evaluation by the researcher. Along with this the students were assessed using various tools and performance tasks. The assessment also included concept mapping and reflective questioning. As mentioned earlier, in the control group the teacher played the main role – explaining, demonstrating, showing audio-visual aids etc. But rarely chances were provided to students to engage in learning.

The studies reviewed include teaching of concepts of newtonian physics (Ibrahim, 2001); Acids and Bases (Terrance, 2001); Nutrition (Banet & Nunez, 1997); Mechanics (Sherri,1995) which may or may not yield to a generalization to learning of others topics effectively. This has been taken care of in the present study. The present study has empirically proved the principles proposed by the above authors (Brooks and Brooks, 1993; Yager, 1991; Steven, 2004) who theoretically emphasized the various factors for improving the achievement of students (as found in Chapter II) by taking seven units covering Biology, Chemistry and Physics.

In the present study, the various instructional inputs including practicing the principles of constructivist method, daily assignments, unit tests conducted, emphasis on practical work and so on had a positive influence over the performance of the students in the achievement test. One of the factors contributed to the results may be continuous assessment and feedback given to the students. The present study qualitatively analysed the reactions of the students, which also gave positive feedback regarding the constructivist approach along with the gain in achievement mean scores obtained. About seventy five percent of the students have shown positive reactions and favoured the constructivist approach as their ideas were encouraged and used by the teacher and also it helped them in learning science content meaningfully. Eighty six percent of the students expressed that the class had democratic atmosphere where in they were given opportunity to talk, discuss, experiment and prove their ideas as correct and so on which also contributed to the improved achievement in science.

During experimentation, the researcher conducted unit tests after completion of every unit. It was found that the students gradually improved from test I to test VII, which indicates the progressive improvement of the students in their conceptual understanding and application of what is learnt among the students. From the responses of reaction scale given by the students, it was found that seventy five percent of them found the evaluation items challenging. They even expressed that the daily assignments in the form of work sheets, hands-on-assignments and periodical testing, etc. also helped them in achieving better.

The study also proved that the Constructivist approach was effective in bringing about a change in the perceptions of students on nature of science ($F = 44.894$; $P<0.00$), between the experimental group and control group, where the mean score of the experimental group (20.97) was found to be higher than the control group (16.28). The change of scores from pretest to post test in perception of nature of science test was 6.03 and 1.94 for experimental and control groups respectively. This finding is concomitant with the findings of Blunck and Yager (1990), which also evidenced that students in classes taught with constructivist approach improved more in their understanding of the nature of science when compared to students in classes taught with a textbook oriented approach. Inturn, Adams (1997) in his study found that the students taught by constructivist model were found to have perceived science as a relevant and useful to every day experience and also appreciated the importance of empirical evidence.

The present findings prove that when the students are given enough opportunities to perform activities and take initiative in exploring science, it not only brings right perceptions of science in students, but also lead to development of science process skills among them. The study also evidenced that constructivist approach as a better method in fostering the development of process skills (F = 99.188; P<.000). The mean score of the experimental group (25.47) was found to be significantly higher than that of the mean score of the control group (19.62). The change of scores from pretest to post science process skill test were 8.86 and 0.78 for experimental and control group respectively. Research evidenced that constructivist approach was effective in fostering science process skills like observation, encouraging hypotheses and their testing, comparing. (Hyang-Lim, 1995); observing, measuring, classifying, interpreting, drawing conclusions (Brass & Duke, 1995). Very few studies were conducted on the development of reasoning skill as an effect of constructivist approach. Hyang- Lim (1995) evidenced that the teacher interventions have promoted progress in reasoning about water dynamics among the younger children. The results of the present study revealed that constructivist approach is effective in fostering reasoning skills along with observing, inferring, predicting, interpreting and hypothesizing.

A highly significant difference in scientific attitude was observed between experimental and control groups (F = 47.215; P<. 000) after the treatments, where mean score of the experimental group (125.02) was found significantly higher than that of the control group (114.50). The change of mean scores from pretest to post test were 8.39 and 4.04 for experimental and control groups respectively.

Very few studies were found where in scientific attitude was considered as one of the consequence variable as an effect of constructivist approach (Preece & Baxter 2000), it is found that not all dimensions of scientific attitude were studied.The above study considered only two dimensions – pseudo beliefs and superstitions. Whereas the present study included 7 dimensions to have a wholistic picture. The study revealed that there exists gender difference with respect to scientific attitude. Females were found less skeptical that the males. In the similar way, the studies conducted in India have also shown marked difference between girls and boys in scientific attitude. It was found interesting to find out whether there is any difference in scientific attitude with respect to gender in the context of constructivist approach in Indian context. This research gap is incorporated in the present study.

It was also found that gender had main effect only on scientific attitude (F = 4.959; P<. 030). Girls (12.94) were found to have improved favourable scientific attitude than boys (11.71) as a reult of constructivist approach.

The reason for improved favorable attitude of girls may be due to rise in socio economic conditions, equal opportunities in school, awareness among the parents and teachers, gender sensitization programmes through media, Information technology, etc. In turn, they helped in reducing gender inequality among people.

The interviews held with some of the students also revealed that they found the constructivist approach very interesting as they were involved most of the times in activities through which they understood quite a many concepts, principles etc. Many times, during the class the students were allowed to experiment and discover things on their own. The students used to repeat the experiment number of times until they arrived at a solution. During this process, the students developed an attitude of objectivity, rationality and willingness to suspend judgment when empirical evidence is obtained. The mean difference and in turn the 't' values were found in the following order in the experimental group: free from superstitions (t = 5.48) > curiousity (t = 5.06) > rationality (t = 4.21) > perseverance (t = 3.83) > willingness to suspend judgement (t = 3.57) > open-mindedness (t = 0.916).

The study also evidenced a highly significant difference in the attitude of students towards science after the treatments given(F = 20.748; P<.000) where mean score of the experimental group (215.67) is found to be significantly higher than that of the control group (194.88). The change of scores from pre to post test were 17.25 and 3.85 for experimental and control groups respectively. Blunck and Yager (1990), Sherri (1996), Yore (1997) and Pooran (2000) also found that constructivist approach developed a positive attitude towards science among the students in their investigation. In turn, it was also found that the favourable attitude towards science led to high science achievement among the students. They examined the effects of constructivist learning environment on attitude towards science compared to students enrolled in a traditional course. The constructivist course utilized cooperative grouping and learning with very little lecture method. Quantitatively, students said that they enjoyed science learning more due to constructivist strategies, teacher's interaction, hands on experiences provided. The experimental group subjects were found to have high positive attitudes than their counter parts.

It was revealed from analysis that constructivist approach was found equally effective for both boys and girls with respect to their perception of nature of science, science process skills and attitude towards science. More over, it was also found that there is no interaction effect of gender and group on perception of nature of science, science process skills and attitude towards science. Where as in the case of achievement in science, there was no main effect of gender, but when interacted with the group found to have significant effect ($F = 10.777; P < .002$). The girls (24.00) belonging to the experimental group gained better than the other groups. In contrast to these findings, Pooran (2000) found that there was no significant interaction effects obtained for method of instruction (Constructivist approach) by gender.

This is attributed to the treatment given to the students of experimental group. The treatment exposed the students to various methods like experimentation, reflective questioning, film shows, field trips, role-plays etc. might have contributed to the higher achievement, skills and favorable attitudes.

Most of the students' expressions revealed during the interview was found highly positive about constructivist approach. One of the student's expressions transcripted is as follows.

"Previously we used to cram the answers and write in the tests but this new method of learning, daily assignments, including variety of exercises, various type of test items in unit tests helped us in improving our science learning. Now I feel science as a very interesting subject, it is not just knowledge, but it is a route to find knowledge and helps in finding solutions to problems. It was very difficult to us to answer them because the assignments many times were out of the text book, so we went to library, we used to discuss with the teacher about the sources. Like this,

we were very busy through out the class. We were allowed to explore in the natural environment. We had participated in various activities like projects, experimentation, collection of various leaves in a field trip, watching films, played various games, played role plays and so on. Among them, we liked the role-plays most. We took the role of scientists, we understood the nature of science and as well as scientists during role play. This method gave us a scope to relook into our ideas and correct them in time".

The findings of the study regarding the relationship between the variables, namely achievement in science, perception of nature of science, science process skills, scientific attitude and attitude towards science showed a positive relationship among all the variables. It is evident from the correlation coefficient value obtained (0.695) that achievement in science and perception of nature of science is positively related to each other. It may be interpreted that the better perception of nature of science will lead to better achievement in science as they are positively related to each other.

The study also indicated a positive correlation between science process skills and achievement in science ($r = 0.696$). The students explored the environment by observing, measuring, hypothesizing, predicting, interpreting, inferring and in turn acquired knowledge. Thus, it can be explained as the greater the development of science process skills, greater will be the achievement in science. It was also revealed that Scientific attitude($r = 0.649$) and attitude towards science ($r = 0.456$) are positively related to achievement in science. The process skills along with attitudes help in raising the achievement level of the students.

Correlation analysis also revealed that the perception of nature of science is positively related to science process skills ($r = 0.598$; $P < .000$), scientific attitude ($r = 0.599$; $P < .000$) and attitude towards science ($r = 0.424$; $P < .000$). The correlation coefficients also indicate that a significant positive relation exists between science process skills and scientific attitude($r = 0.668$; $P < .000$) and also attitude towards science ($r = 0.508$; $P < .000$). The studies conducted by Blunck and Yager (1990), Sherri (1996), Yore (1997) and Pooran (2000) also supported the above findings.

An empirical finding of this kind not only strengthens the belief that constructivist approach helps in better understanding of scientific knowledge and sharpening of cognitive skills, but also necessitates a need for further in-depth research into many influencing factors associated with learning.

Conclusion

In this chapter the data was analyzed and interpreted under different sections. The study indicated improvement of students in their achievement in science, perception of nature of science, science process skills, scientific attitude and attitude towards science among secondary level students as a result of the Constructivist approach. This result is also attributed to the positive relation among all the above variables. The Qualitative data obtained from the reaction scale and interviews also support the interpretation and point out to the success of Constructivist approach, which is realized in terms of its effect on the variables mentioned.

In the next chapter the summary and major findings of the study are presented.

5

Summary and Conclusions

Genesis of the Problem

"Science is what the scientist does. It is a process by which we increase and refine understanding ourselves and of the universe through continuous observation, experimentation, application and verification" Gagne (1965).

Science thus, is simultaneously, a body of knowledge and a way of gaining and using that knowledge. The accumulated and systematized body of knowledge, which is the 'product' of science-has a dynamic counterpart, the scientific attitudes and methods of inquiry—which is the 'process' of science. Scientific attitudes include both emotional attitudes such as curiousity, humility, determination and open mindedness and intellectual attitudes namely objectivity, skepticism and rationality. Scientific attitude is "the cognitive attitude or belief about thinking and has also affective and behavioral aspects"(Guilford, 1967). Whereas, attitude towards science according to Duckworth (1975) refers to the "disposition of mind for or against scientists, scientific activity and learning of science" and has predominantly affective orientation.

The methods of inquiry are observing, hypothesizing, analyzing, inferring, extrapolating, reasoning, synthesizing etc. In science, the ways of thinking, measuring, solving problems and using thoughts are called processes. Process skills describe the type of thinking and reasoning required. The scientific attitude develops simultaneously with the process skills and with the discovery or construction of useful scientific knowledge.

Learning of science in schools augments the spirit of enquiry, creativity and objectivity along with aesthetic sensibility (National Curricular Framework for School Education, 2000). It aims to develop well-defined abilities of knowing, doing and being. It also nurtures the ability to explore and seek solution to the problems related to the environment and daily life situations and to question the existing beliefs, prejudices and practices in society. Thus, science is must for every child to learn as it gives an opportunity to learn how to learn. The inclusion of science as a discipline and improvement in the science education is the successful effort of various committees and commissions.

The aims and objectives that were laid down were not implemented up to the mark. In this connection, National Science Education Standards (1996) emphasized changes in the teaching and content standards. At national level, NCERT has brought out the National Curriculum Framework for School Education (2000) that viewed child as a constructor of knowledge. It also recommended the development of scientific attitudes, values, critical, creative and generative thinking among the students and also felt a need of exposure to the nature and structure of science. Overall, there expressed a shift of emphasis from information based and teacher-centered education to process centered and learner friendly education.

The present science education is far away from the above vision. In the conventional classroom, the classes are usually driven by "teacher talk" and depend heavily on textbooks for the structure of the course. Teachers serve as pipelines and seek to transfer their thoughts and meanings to the passive students. There is little room for student initiated questions and independent thought or interaction between the students. Overall, it was found that the teachers do not concentrate on the process of learning by students and also overlook the misconceptions among them.

All the above ideas and processes occur repeatedly in constructivist writings. Insights from review revealed that there are innumerable studies conducted on constructivism in west in various disciplines like mathematics, language learning, music, internet learning and so on. It was also tried out in the context of open education. Constructivist approach was tried out at different levels from early childhood education to university level. In India it is yet to gain prominence not only at the research level but even at level of awareness.

Thus, it is felt necessary to study the effectiveness of constructivist approach in improving the science achievement and associated skills in Indian context at secondary level.

Statement of the Problem

The present investigation is titled as

"Effectiveness of constructivist approach on students' achievement in science, scientific attitude and perception of nature of science at secondary level".

Objectives of the Study

With an insight into the philosophical, psychological and pedagogical bases of constructivism, the research undertaken aimed to study a few research bearing questions, which may throw more light upon constructivism as an approach to learning. These are reflected in the form of objectives given below:

1. To develop science lessons based on constructivist approach in the selected units of science for eighth standard students.
2. To study the effectiveness of constructivist approach on the students' achievement in science.
3. To study the effectiveness of constructivist approach on the students' perception of nature of science.
4. To study the effectiveness of constructivist approach in developing science process skills among the students.
5. To study the effectiveness of constructivist approach in developing scientific attitude among the students.
6. To study the effectiveness of constructivist approach on the students' attitude towards science.

7. To study the interaction between 'gender' and 'group' with reference to achievement in science, perception of nature of science, scientific attitude, science process skills and attitude towards science.

8. To examine the relationship among achievement in science, perception of nature of science, science process skills, scientific attitude and attitude towards science.

Hypotheses Formulated for the Study

The following research hypotheses were formulated in pursuance of the broad objectives of the study:

H1: The constructivist approach does have a positive effect on the achievement of students in science.

H2: The constructivist approach does have a positive effect on the students' perception of nature of science.

H3: The constructivist approach does have a positive effect on the development of science process skills in students.

H4: The constructivist approach does have a positive effect on the scientific attitude of students.

H5: The constructivist approach does have a positive effect on the students' attitude towards science.

H7: There is an interaction between 'gender' and 'group' on students' achievement in science, perception of nature of science, scientific attitude, science process skills and attitude towards science.

H9: There is a positive relationship among achievement in science, perception of nature of science, science process skills, scientific attitude and attitude towards science.

The Design of the Study

The present investigation was carried out to study the effectiveness of constructivist approach in science. The study was quasi experimental in nature. Quasi-experimental designs provide a relatively high degree of experimental-control in natural settings and they clearly represent a step-up from pre-experimental designs because they enable researchers to compare the performance of the experimental group with that of a control group.

Non-equivalent control group design was adopted in the present study, which is similar to the pretest-posttest control group design except for the absence of the random selection of students from a population and random assignment of the students to the experimental and control groups.

Sampling Procedure

The purposive sampling technique was used in the present study. The two schools namely Demonstration Multipurpose School, RIE, Mysore and Kendriya Vidyalaya, Mysore of Karnataka State were selected for the study. The eighth standard students belonging to Demonstration Multipurpose School were treated as experimental group where as the students of Kendriya Vidyalaya were treated as control group.

Sample for the Study

The intact groups of sixty-eight eighth standard students in total including both experimental and control group were taken up for the study. The sample included 37 boys and 31 girls in total.

The experimental group (Demonstration Multipurpose School) consisted of 36 eighth standard students, of which were 21 boys and 15 girls and the control group (Kendriya Vidyalaya, Mysore) consisted 32 students, which included 16 boys and 16 girls.

Procedural Details of the Study

The study was carried out in three phases: the developmental phase; try out phase and validation/implementation phase.

Phase I- Developmental Phase

At this stage, along with the instructional materials including lesson plans, activity sheets, unit tests; the tools namely achievement test in science, perception of nature of science test, science process skills test, scientific attitude scale, attitude towards science scale and reaction scale were developed.

Development of the Instructional Materials Based on Constructivist Model

After the selection of content, the content analysis was done to identify concepts, teaching points, science process skills, attitudes, values etc. The lesson plans were prepared making use of 4E's Model i.e Exploration, Explanation, Expansion and Evaluation. The lessons were planned focusing on building better perception of nature of science, scientific attitude and gave emphasis on development of science process skills. Worksheets, concept maps, projects, unit tests etc. were planned and prepared.

Tools Used/Developed in the Study

The description of the tools used in the study is given below

i. Ravens Progressive Matrices

Ravens progressive matrices was made use of to know the mental ability of the students. The test is made up of five sets of diagrammatic puzzles exhibiting serial changes in two dimensions simultaneously. Each puzzle has a part missing, which the person taking the test has to find among the options provided.

The standard test consists of sixty problems divided into five sets (A, B, C, D, and E) each made up of 12 problems. Each correct answer was given one mark. The total raw score was found and it is used as a covariate in the present study.

The test-retest reliabilities reported by the authors Stinissen, Dolke, Sheppart and Goetzinger, range from 0.80 to 0.93 and Internal consistency reliabilities reported, range from 08.87 to 0.97 (Blansk and Sinha , Elley and Mac Arthur King, Laroche and Bruke).

ii. Achievement Test in Science

The pre- and post-achievement levels of students of experimental and control groups were measured by using the achievement test, designed by the investigator. A comprehensive achievement test was developed covering seven units of eighth standard syllabus including natural and physical sciences. The objectives covered in this test comprised knowledge, understanding, application and the skill. The achievement test consisted of 60 items, including 36 multiple-choice items, 8 fill in the blanks and 16 short answered questions with the allocation of sixty marks on the whole.

The test-retest reliability method was used to establish reliability for all the tools. The correlation coefficient value (r=0.9) indicated the achievement test as highly reliable.

iii. Perception of Nature of Science Test

Perception of nature of science test was developed to know the perceptions of students on nature of science. Perception of nature of science of students was pertaining to the following aspects namely:

1. Characteristics of Science;
2. Scientific methods/processes;
3. Use of scientific discoveries;
4. Application of science in daily life; and
5. Role of science in society and its impact on human beings.

Twenty-six items including objective as well as descriptive items were included in the perception of nature of science test. It was found to be reliable with the correlation coefficient value of 0.7.

iv. Science Process Skills Test

This test was developed to assess the science process skills developed among the eighth standard students. The process skills test comprised of thirtysix multiple choice items with four alternatives measuring the following selected process skills namely:

1. Observing;
2. Inferring;
3. Hypothesizing;
4. Predicting;
5. Interpreting; and
6. Reasoning.

The science process skills test was found to be highly reliable with the test-retest reliability coefficient (0.95).

v. **Scientific Attitude Scale**

This scale was used to measure the scientific attitude among the secondary school students. Among Grinnell's twenty components of scientific attitude (as discussed in chapter one), only seven were taken for the present study namely:

1. Objectivity;
2. Curiosity;
3. Open-mindedness;
4. Perseverance;
5. Rationality;
6. Free from superstitions; and
7. Willingness to suspend judgment.

This scale was developed using both Likert's scale and situational testing. The scientific attitude scale comprises of forty-four items including twenty-two Likert type items rated on five points and twenty-two situational test items with three options.

The test-retest reliability coefficient value obtained was 0.66, which indicated the test as reliable.

vi. **Attitude Towards Science Scale**

This attitude scale was developed to find out the effectiveness of constructivist approach on students' attitude towards science on a five-point Likert rating scale. The attitude of students was measured towards the elements, namely:

1. Using science materials to do science activities (investigative process);
2. Perceived comfort or discomfort related to classroom science;
3. Learning science content;
4. Reading or talking about science related topics; and
5. Viewing science programmes on films or T.V.

The attitude scale contained 44 items measuring students' attitude towards the above elements.

This test was found to be reliable with test-retest reliability coefficient of 0.65.

vii. Reaction Scale

A reaction scale was constructed to know pupils' reactions towards constructivist approach adopted in teaching science towards the following four main components namely:

1. The method used;
2. The classroom atmosphere;
3. The role of teacher; and
4. The evaluation techniques used.

The reaction scale contained 35 objective and 6 open-ended questions. The objective type items were framed in the question form, which can be answered on a three point scale i.e. Yes/ Sometimes/No.

viii. Semi-Structured Interview

Interviews were taken to elicit the views of students on treatment given to them. General interview guide approach was used for conducting the interview. This approach essentially involves having an outline of topics to be covered during an interview; however, the order in which the topics is addressed is not set. The questions are not formulated beforehand. Interview guide focused the data collection in four topics or areas namely:

1. Teaching using constructivist approach;
2. Classroom climate;
3. Role of teacher; and
4. Evaluation techniques.

Each student was given opportunity to reply the questions in the same categories. The time limit for an interview ranged from 20-25 minutes.

Phase II-Try Out Phase

The instructional materials prepared and the tools constructed were tried out on the eighth standard students of local schools.

Phase III- Implementation Phase

The present study is a quasi-experimental study involving a non-equivalent pre-test and posttest design. In this design, the effects of the treatments were judged by the difference between the pretest and post test scores. This is compared with the control group. This phase was carried out in three stages:

Administration of Pretests

The students of both the experimental and control groups were simultaneously pre tested on Ravens progressive matrices, achievement test in science, perception of nature of science test, science process skills test, scientific attitude scale and attitude towards science scale one by one. One test was given each day for both the groups to avoid fatigue.

Implementation of Experiment/Treatment

The instructional materials developed were implemented to the experimental group for a period of four months. Consulting the science teacher of control group, the duration i.e. number of periods required for teaching the selected lessons was decided. The investigator taught seven units using constructivist approach to the experimental group. Classes were taken in their regular science periods and also when any regular teacher was absent. Some times even co-curricular activity periods were made use of for conducting laboratory experiments (approximately 150 periods). In the control group, classes were taken by their regular science teacher and covered the portion approximately in the same number of periods. It was observed by the investigator that the regular science teacher used alternate strategy like lecture method, charts etc., for teaching the selected seven lessons for the control group. The investigator got continuous feedback from the experimental group students and their regular teachers. The lessons were also audio recorded which added up to the feedback. A unit test was given as soon as each lesson was completed apart from daily assignments.

Administering of Post-tests

After the completion of the treatments, both the experimental and control group were post tested on achievement test in science, scientific attitude scale, perception of nature of science test, science process skills test and attitude towards science scale. Apart from the above tests, a reaction scale was given and interviews were conducted to the experimental group students to get their reaction towards the experimental treatment, teacher and the evaluation techniques used.

Statistical Techniques Employed

The following statistical techniques were used to analyse the collected data.

i. Student 't' Test

't' test was used to know the significance of difference between pretest and posttest of various levels of objectives in an achievement test, dimensions of science process skills and scientific attitude.

ii. Pearson's Product Moment Correlation

This technique was used to find out the correlation among achievement in science, perception of nature of science, science process skills, scientific attitude and attitude towards science.

iii. Analysis of Covariance Test

As the design of the study demanded controlling the initial differences between experimental and control groups, analysis of covariance was employed. Univariate procedure provides regression analysis and analysis of variance for one dependent variable by one or more factors. It not only gives the effects of other variables on the mean scores of the various groupings of the dependent variable, but also the interactions between factors and as well as the individual factors. In addition, the effects of covariates and covariate interactions with factors are included.

Analysis of Data

The data collected on all the tests were analysed both descriptively and inferentially. The SPSS (10.0 version) was made use of for the statistical analysis of data. Pre-test score and intelligence score were taken as covariates to control the initial differences between experimental and control group. The analysis on achievement as a whole and also content and objective-wise was done. The daily assignments and the unit tests, which were conducted, were analysed to see the improvement in the science achievement among the students of experimental group. In the same way, the effectiveness of constructivist approach was also found out on all the variables namely perception of nature of science, science process skills, scientific attitude and attitude towards science. The component-wise analysis was performed for scientific attitude and process skills to find out which component was more influenced by constructivist approach. The interaction effect of gender with the treatments on all the variables was studied. Along with effectiveness of constructivist approach on the dependent variable, the relationship among the variables was also examined.

The reactions expressed by the students towards the constructivist approach in the reaction scale and in the interviews conducted were analysed and reported qualitatively.

Major Findings of the Study

1. Constructivist approach was found effective in improving the achievement in science, perception of nature of science, science process skills, scientific attitude and attitude towards science among eighth standard students. This is evident from the F values obtained for treatments.

2. Constructivist approach was found equally effective for both girls and boys in improving their achievement in science, perception of nature of science, science process skills and attitude towards science.

3. There is a significant difference in scientific attitude of girls and boys. Girls seem to have scored better than boys on scientific attitude scale.

4. There is a significant interaction between 'gender' and 'groups' on achievement in science wherein girls (24.00) belonging to experiment group have gained better than that of boys.

5. There is a non-significant interaction between 'gender' and 'groups' on perception of nature of science, science process skills, scientific attitude and attitude towards science.

6. There is a significant difference in the attainment of levels of objectives (Knowledge, Understanding, Application and Skill) in achievement in science as an effect of constructivist approach. The 't' values for the pretest and post-test of knowledge, understanding, application and skill level were found to be 8.135, 18.214, 10.959 and 9.659 respectively and were found to be significant at 0.01 level. Among the four levels of objectives, the 't' values of understanding and application level were predominantly high.

7. There is a significant difference in the development of various selected science process skills as an effect of constructivist approach. Among the six process skills the 't' value for inferring was found to be greater in experiment group. The acquisition of science process skills were found in the order of inferring (11.879)> reasoning (9.723)> hypothesizing (9.619)> interpreting (6.817)> observing (5.351)> predicting (4.781). Even though the 't' value for observing was less but improvement in the other process skills of hypothesizing, predicting and inferring subsumes the skill of observation that is basic to all other skills.

8. There is a significant difference in the development of the various selected dimensions of the scientific attitude of students. This is evident from the 't' values. The 't' value for free from superstitions (5.45) was greater than all other dimensions of scientific attitude.

   The mean difference and in turn the 't' values were found in the following order in the experiment group: free from superstitions (5.48) > curiousity (5.06) > rationality (4.21) > objectivity (4.210) > perseverance (3.83) > willingness to suspend judgement (3.57) > open-mindedness (0.916).

9. Among all the variables there is a great change in the scores from pretest to post-test in the achievement in science of students belonging to experimental group (20.80). There is 34.65 percent raise in the achievement of students.

10. There is a positive relationship among achievement in science, perception of nature of science, science process skills, scientific attitude and attitude towards science with each other.

11. The following conclusions about constructivist approach were arrived at from the observations and reactions expressed by the students:

    (i) Out of 36 students, thirty-four (94.4%) of them liked the new method i.e. constructivist approach and also expressed that this approach helped them in learning the science content meaningfully.

    (ii) Apart from knowledge construction, certain qualities like working cooperatively in a group, peer understanding and adjustment and also in building self-confidence had strengthened during learning process.

    (iii) The teacher provided democratic classroom atmosphere, which not only provided the students an opportunity to talk, discuss, experiment and prove their ideas as correct but also helped in learning better. It also gave an opportunity in improving good relationship among the students and with the teacher.

    (iv) The new innovative evaluation techniques used were very interesting, challenging and highly motivating.

Educational Implications of the Study

The following are the educational implications of the present study:

1. This study highlights the shift from teacher centered to learner-centered classroom wherein the students are given complete freedom to explore and discover things on their own. The role of a teacher is just a facilitator and guide. This study could really be very useful to the teachers in creating innovative classroom situations wherein the students are meaning makers which is the ultimate aim of learning.

2. It is found that constructivist approach is more effective than the conventional method of teaching science in fostering

achievement in science. In this method, the learner comes to learning situations with knowledge gained from previous experience and that prior knowledge influences what new or modified knowledge they will construct from new learning experiences. It emphasizes learning through meaning making process rather than memorization of concepts. So, this method can be practiced in the schools to facilitate meaningful learning among the students.

3. This study focuses the change in the trend of teaching from transmission of knowledge from enlightened to unenlightened in constructing the meanings of the concepts based on the prerequisite knowledge. This study also emphasized the importance of a variety of learning experiences to advance different levels of learning.

4. This study also gives a picture of an innovative and democratic classroom where in the priority is given to the students' autonomy and the relationship between students and teacher and among the students. It was revealed that the students have really enjoyed the classroom experience and also felt that this method was not at all stressful. This study paved a pathway for a healthy classroom, which led to healthy relationship among the students and also with the teacher.

5. This study also revealed that the students liked group works and also expressed that they got an opportunity to discuss and share with each other and added to this, the constructivist philosophy believes in both individual and group construction of knowledge. So, the teachers have to provide both individual and group works to the students while teaching in the classroom.

6. The constructivist approach is an effective method in building up better perception of nature of science among the students, which is one of the main objectives of science education. It was also evident that there is a positive relation among perception of nature of science, achievement in science, science process skills, scientific attitude and attitude towards science, which stresses the importance of perception of nature

of science. Thus, this study throws light on the importance of perception of nature of science among the students and the role of teacher in enhancing it. So, the higher authorities along with the teachers should provide the opportunities to the students in understanding science.

7. In this study, it was found that constructivist approach was effective in developing science process skills among the students. During the treatment the students were given opportunity to develop the skills of observing, hypothesizing, reasoning and were also encouraged to connect and summarize concepts by analyzing, predicting, justifying and defend their ideas. From the results of this study, it is suggested that the teachers should provide suitable learning situations wherein the students get a first hand experience of handling the equipment, making use of senses, explore and experiment and lastly, infer the results.

8. As the model requires active participation throughout the class, it not only helps in improving achievement, attitudes namely scientific attitude and attitude towards science, but also helps in improving their language ability. Thus, it is suggested that the teachers should provide conducive environment in building favourable attitudes.

9. Training programmes on constructivist approach could be organized for pre-service and in-service teachers so as to develop an understanding and the necessary skills for the successful implementation of the model in the classroom situation.

10. The higher authorities DIETs, State departments of education should include constructivist method of teaching in the teacher training programmes. The student teachers are to be taught with the theory of constructivism and should be allowed to practice during their practice in teaching.

Suggestions for Further Research

1. A qualitative study could be taken up to understand the process of construction of meanings among the students of secondary level.

2. Similar studies could be conducted with a larger sample and on students of classes VII, IX and X.
3. The sample considered for the present study is urban sample following CBSE (Central Board of Secondary Education) pattern. The experiment can be tried on rural sample and also on students of schools following state syllabus.
4. A comparative study could be taken up to find out the effectiveness of constructivist approach between a rural and an urban sample.
5. A comparative study of individual constructivism and social constructivism could be taken up on secondary level students.
6. A study could be undertaken to examine the characteristics and role of teachers in constructivist classrooms.
7. Studies could be undertaken to develop valid and reliable tools for assessing the scientific attitude and perception of nature of science for the secondary level.
8. Similar studies could be taken up to investigate the effectiveness of constructivist approach in different school subjects like language, social studies and mathematics.
9. It is felt that the students of different socio-economic levels, personalities might differ in responding to the constructivist approach. So, studies to investigate the interaction effects of constructivist approach with other variables such as SES, age, personality factors and development of scientific attitude, science process skills and achievement in science could be taken up.
10. Studies to develop training strategies for teachers in constructivist approach, to develop competencies and attitude in handling the model could be taken up.
11. An evaluative study of attitudes of teachers and students on constructivist approach as a teaching strategy could be considered.

12. A constructivist based instructional approach to help secondary level students to improve all the elements of scientific literacy could be taken up.

13. Study to investigate the influence of interactive constructivist instructional model on attitude towards science could be undertaken.

14. Studies could be undertaken to examine the student perceptions of the constructivist classroom.

15. The present study included the selected science process skills namely observing, hypothesizing, predicting, reasoning, inferring and interpreting. So, studies could be taken up to study the effectiveness of constructivist approach on all the remaining science process skills.

Bibliography

AAAS (1990). Science for All Americans. New York, NY: Oxford University Press.

Abd-El-Khalick, F., Bell, R.L., and Lederman, N.G. (1998). The Nature of Science and Instructional Practice: Making the Unnatural Natural. *Science Education*, 82(4), 417-437.

Adams (1997). Students' Beliefs, Attitudes and Conceptual Change in a Traditional and Constructivistic High School Physics Classroom. *Dissertation Abstracts International*, 58(8), 3069-A, 1998.

Akindehin, F. (1988). Effect of An Instructional Package on Preservice Science Teachers' Understanding of the Nature of Science and Acquisition of Science-related Attitudes. *Science Education*, 72(1), 73-82.

Aldridge, F.M., Fraser, B.F. and Taylor, P.C. (2000). Constructivist Learning Environments in a Cross-national Study in Taiwan and Australia. *International Journal of Science Education*, 22(1), 37-55.

Allen, L.B. (2001). The Construction of Personal Meaning in the Transformation of a School's Culture: Three Journeys Along the Pathway of School Improvement. *Dissertation Abstracts International*, 61(11), 4244-A, 2001.

Allport, G.W. (1955). Attitudes. In Murchinson (Ed.). *Handbook of Social Psychology.* Worlster, Mass: Clark University Press.

American Association for the Advancement of Science (1993). *Benchmarks for Science Literacy.* New York: Oxford University Press.

Amos, S. and Boohan, R. (2002). *Aspects of Teaching Secondary Science Perspectives on Practice.* Routledge, London: Falmer Press.

Anderson, R.D., et. al. (1970). *Developing Children's Thinking Through Science.* Englewood Cliffs, New Jersey: Prentice Hall.

Anyanchi, Carolyn, M.E. (1996). Teaching Science in Nigerian Secondary Schools Using a Constructivist Model. *Dissertation Abstracts International,* 58(4), 1237-A, 1997.

Appleton, K. (1993). Using Theory to Guide Practice: Teaching Science from a Constructivist Perspective. *School Science and Mathematics,* 93(5), 270.

Appleton, K. (1997). Analysis and Description of Students' Learning During Science Classes Using a Constructivist-based Model. *Journal of Research in Science Teaching,* 34(3), 303-318.

Appleton, Ken and Asoko, Hilary (1996). A Case Study of a Teachers' Progress Toward Using a Constructivist View of Learning to Inform Teaching in Elementary Science. *Science Education,* 80(2), 165-180.

Ausubel, D.P. (1968). Educational Psychology: A Cognitive View, New York: Holt, Rinehart and Winston.

Ausubel, D. (1968). *Educational Psychology. A Cognitive View.* New York: Holt, Rinehart and Winston. pp. 83-84.

Baker, D.R. and Piburn, M. (1991). Process Skills Acquisition, Cognitive Growth, and Attitude Change of Ninth Grade Students in a Scientific Literacy Course. *Journal of Research in Science Teaching,* 28(5), pp. 423-436.

Banet, E. and Nunez, F. (1997). Teaching and Learning About Human Nutrition: A Constructivist Approach. *International Journal of Science Education,* 19(10), 1169-1194.

Barnard, D.J. et. al. (1962). *Science: A Search for Evidence.* Macmillan Science-Life Series a Total Programme in Science.

Barnard, Darrell J, et. al. (1959). *The New Basic Science.* New York: Macmillan Company.

Baylor, Samsonov and Smith. (eds.) (1996). *A Collaborative Class Investigation into Telecommunications in Education:* Constructivism, EDTC 618 On-Line Reader.

Beard, L.J.A. (1995). An Investigation and Analysis of Secondary Science Teachers' Perceptions of the Constructivist Theory. *Dissertation Abstracts International,* 56(7), 2546-A, 1996.

Bednarshi, Marsha H. (1998). Constructivism and the Use of Performance Assessment in Science: A Comparative Study of Beliefs Among Pre-service and In-service Teachers. *Dissertation Abstracts International,* 58(8), 1998.

Beeth, M.E., et. al. (2001). A Continuum for Assessing Science Process Knowledge in Grades K-6. *Electronic Journal of Science Education,* 5(3).

Behrendt, H. et. al., (ed.). (2001). *Research in Science Education-Past, Present and Future.* London: Kluwer Academic Publishers.

Black, J.B. and R.O. Mc. Clintock. (1995). An Interpretation Construction Approach to Constructivist Design. In B.Wilson (Ed.) *Constructivist Learning Environments.* Engle Wood Cliffs, NJ: Educational Technology Publications.

Bloom, B. (1979). *Human Characteristics and School Learning.* New York: McGraw-Hill.

Blunck, S.M. and Yager, R.E. (1990). The Iowa Chautauqua Programme: A Model for Improving Science in the Elementary School. *Journal of Elementary Science Education,* 2(2), 3-9.

Boden, M.A. (1979). *Piaget. Outline and Critique of his Psychology, Biology and Philosophy.* Harvester Press.

Brandwein P.F., et. al., (1958). *Teaching High School Science. A Book of Methods.* New York: Harcourt, Brace & World, Inc.

Brandwein, P.F., et. al., (1966). *Concepts in Science.* New York: Harcourt, Brace & World, Inc.

Brooks J.G. and Brooks M.G. (1993). In Search of Understanding: The Case for Constructivism Classrooms. Alexandria VA: Association for Supervision and Curriculum Development.

Brooks, M.G and Brooks, J.C. (1999). The Courage to be Constructivist. *Educational Leadership,* 57(3).

Brown and Thomas John (2000). What Students are Saying About Science: Student Perspectives of Meaningful, Effective and Ineffective Learning Experiences in Science Class. *Dissertation Abstracts International,* 61(10), 3944-A, 2001.

Caprio, M.W. (1994). Easing into Constructivism, Connecting Meaningful Learning with Student Experience. *Journal of College Science Training,* 23(4), 210-212.

Carin, A.A. and Sund, R.B. (1964). *Teaching Science Through Discovery.* Columbus, Ohio: Charles E. Merrill Publishing Company, A Bell & Howell Company.

Chaille, C. and Britain, L. (1991). *The Young Child As Scientist: A Constructivist Approach to Early Childhood Science Education.* New York: Harper Collins Publishers Inc.

Chi-Der, C. (2000). Constructivism in General Music Education. A Music Teachers Live Experience. *Dissertation Abstracts International,* 61(5), 1726-A, 2000.

Choksi, N.P. (2004). Constructivism: New Vision for Learning of Modern Era. Paper Presented at 17th Annual Conference of All India Association for Educational Research as International Conference on Fourth Wave Education, Saurashtra University, Rajkot. Jan. 10-12.

Chotalia, M. (2004). De-paradigming Education: Peering Beyond Constructivism. Paper Presented at 17th Annual Conference of All India Association for Educational Research as International Conference on Fourth Wave Education, Saurashtra University, Rajkot. Jan. 10-12.

Christianson, R.G. (1999). Comparison of Student Learning About Diffusion and Osmosis in Constructivist and Traditional Classrooms. *International Journal of Science Education*, 21(6), 687-698.

Clemens, J.L.M. (2001). The Students Experience in a Constructivist Classroom. *Dissertation Abstracts International*, 62(5), 2001.

Cobb, T. (1999). Applying Constructivism: A Test for the Learner as Scientist. *Educational Technology Research and Development*, 47(3), 15-31.

Cobern, W.W. (1996). Constructivist and Non-western Science Education Research. *International Journal of Science Education*, 18(3), 295-310.

Cole, M. and Wertsch, J.V. (1996). Beyond the Individual—Social Antimony in Discussion of Piaget and Vygotsky, *Human development*, 39, 250-256.

Conant, J.B. (1951). *Science and Common Sense*. New Haven, Conn: Yale University Press.

Crowther, D.T. (1997). Science Experiences and Attitudes of Elementary Education Majors As They Experience Biology 295: A Multiple Case Study. *Dissertation Abstracts International*, 57(7), 2952-A, 1999.

Curtis, F.D. and Mallinson, G.G. (1958). *Science in Daily Life*. Ginn & Company.

Cynthia, E.L. (1993). Qualitative Comparison of Students' Constructions of Science. *Science Education*, 77(6), 611-622.

Daigle, Marie A. (2000). The Learner-centered Classroom: Helping Teachers Apply Constructivist Principles to Standards-based Teaching and Assessment. Paper Presented at the Annual Meeting of the Association for the Education of Teachers of Science.

Damon, Linda, et. al. (1997). Preparing Teachers for Tomorrow: A Constructivist Approach. *ERIC Document Reproduction Service:* No. ED410207.

Dash, N.K. (2002). Implications of Constructivism for Instructional Design in Open and Distance Learning. *University News*, 40(4), 33-38.

Davis, I.C., et. al. (1962). *Science Observation and Experiment*. U.S.A.: Holt Rinchart & Winston Inc.

Desautels Jacques (1998). "Constructivism-in-action: Students Examine Their Idea of Science". In Marie Larochelle, et. al. (ed). *Constructivism and Education*. pp.121-191. Cambridge: Cambridge University Press.

Dewey, J. (1916). *Democracy and Education*. New York: Macmillan, Inc.

Diederich, P.B. (1967). Components of the Scientific Attitude. *The Science Teacher*, 34, 23-24.

Donga, N.S. (2004). Theoretical and Practical Constructivist View of Secondary School Teachers. Paper Presented at 17th Annual Conference of All India Association for Educational Research As International Conference on Fourth Wave Education, Saurashtra University, Rajkot. Jan. 10-12.

Driver, R. and Oldham, V. (1986). A Constructivist Approach to Curriculum Development in Science. *Studies in Science Education*, 13, 105-122.

Driver, R., Asoko, H., Leach, J., Mortimer, E., and Scott, P. (1994). Constructing Scientific Knowledge in the Classroom. *Educational Researcher*, 23(7), 5-12.

Dryden, M. and Fraser, B.J. (1998). Evaluating Urban Systemic Reform Using the Constructivist Learning Environment Survey. A Paper Presented At the Annual Meeting of the American Educational Research Association, San Diego.

Duckworth, E. (1987). The Virtues of not Knowing. In E. Duckworth (Ed.), *The Having of Wonderful Ideas*. (pp. 64-69). New York: Teachers College Press.

Edward, A.L. (1967). *Statistical Methods*. Holt, Richart and Winston Inc.

Edward, A.L. (1969). *Techniques of Attitude Scale Construction*. Bombay: Vakil Kaffer Simpson.

Elaine, K.J. (1996). Constructing a Constructivist Classroom: Knowledge, Learning and Language in Science Education. *Dissertation Abstracts International*, 57(4), 1547-A, 1996.

Elmes, D.G., et. al. (2003). *Research Methods in Psychology*. Wadsworth, Thomson Learning Academic Resource Centre.

Ernest, P. (1995). The One and the Many. In L. Steff and J.Gale (Ed.). *Constructivism in Education* (pp.459-486). New Jersey: Lawrence Erlbaum Associates, Inc.

Feigl, H. and Brodbeck, M. (1953). *Readings in the Philosophy of Science*. New York: Appleton-Century-Crofts.

Fensham, P.J., Gunstone, R.F., and White R.T. (eds.). (1994). *The Content of Science: A Constructivist Approach to its Teaching and Learning*. Washington, D.C.: Falmer press.

Finley, F.N. (1983). Science processes. *Journal of Research in Science Teaching*, 20(1), 47-54.

Forawi and Safian A. Said (1996). The Effects of the Interaction of Teachers' Understanding of the Nature of Science, Instructional Strategy and Textbook on Students' Understanding of the Nature of Science. *Dissertation Abstracts International*, 57(3), 1082-A, 1996.

Forguson (1976). *Statistical Analysis in Psychology and Education* (4th Edition). Tokyo: Mc. Graw Hill, Kogukupha Ltd.

Fosnot, C.T. (1993). Rethinking Science Education: A Defense of Piagetian Constructivism. *Journal of Research in Science Teaching*, 30(9), 1189-1201.

Fosnot, C.T. (1996). *Constructivism: Theory, Perspectives and Practice*. New York: Teachers College, Columbia University.

Foxx, et al. (2001). Evaluation of Constructivist Pedagogy: Influence on Critical Thinking Skills, Science Fair Participation and Level of Performance. *Dissertation Abstracts International*, 62(2), 516-A, 2001.

Fraser, B.J. (1978). Development of a Test of Science-related Attitudes. *Science Education*, 62 (4), 509-515.

Freedman, R.L.H. (1998). Assessment Practices of Iowa Science Teachers from a Constructivist Perspectives, Unpublished Doctoral Dissertation, The University of Iowa City.

Freeman, K., et. al. (1958). *Helping Children Understand Science.* U.S.A.

Furth, H.G. (1969). *Piaget & Knowledge. Theoretical Foundations.* Englewood Cliffs, N.J.: Prentice Hall Inc.

Gagne, R. (1965). *The Conditions of Learning.* New York: Holt, Rinehart and Winston.

Gales and Mary Jane (2000). Relationship Between Constructivist Teacher Beliefs and Instructional Practices to Students' Mathematical Achievement. *Dissertation Abstracts International,* 61(1), 39-A, 2000.

Garret, Henry E. (1954). *Statistics in Psychology and Education,* New York: Longmans, Green and Co., Inc.

Gauld, Colin (1982). The Scientific Attitude and Science Education: A Critical appraisal. *Science Education,* 66(1), 109-121.

Geber, B.A. (ed.). (1977). *Piaget and Knowing.* New York: Routledge & Kegan Paul Limited, Gresham Press.

Gilbert, J.K., Osborne, R. and Fensham, P. (1982). Children's Science and Its Consequences for Teaching. *Science Education,* 66, 623-633.

Gibson, H.L. and Vanstrat, G. (2000). The Impact of Instructional Methods on Preservice Teachers' Attitude Towards Teaching and Learning. Paper Presented at the Annual Meeting of the American Educational Research Association, April 24-28, 2000, New Orleans.

Golden, T. (2003). Assessing the Effects of Traditional and Constructivist Teaching Methodologies on Comprehension of Content of An Acids and Bases Chemistry Unit in the 7th Grade. *Dissertation Abstracts International,* 63(8), 2827-A, 2003.

Goodwin, A. (2001). Wonder in Science Teaching and Learning: An Update. *School Science Review,* 83(302), 69-73.

Gray, W. E. (1994). A Study of the Effects of a Constructivist-based Mathematics Problem Solving Instructional Programme on the Attitudes, Self-confidence and Achievement of Post-fifth Grade Students. *Dissertation Abstracts International*, 55(11), 3411-A, 1995.

Griffard, et. al. (1999). Gaps in College Biology Students Understanding of Photosynthesis: Implications for Human Constructivist Learning Theory and College Classroom Practice. *Dissertation Abstracts International*, 61(2), 552-A, 2000.

Guilford (1978). *Psychometric Methods*. New York: McGraw-Hill Publishers Limited, p. 349.

Gurney, B.F.(1995). Tugboats and Tennis Games: Preservice Conceptions of Training and Learning Revealed Through Metaphors. *Journal of Research in Science Teaching*, 32(6), 569-83.

Habemas, Jurgen (1979). *Communication and Evolution of Society*. Boston: Beacon Press.

Hand, B. and Treagust, D.F. (1994). Teachers Thought About Changing to Constructivist Teaching/Learning Approaches Within Junior Secondary Science Classrooms. *Journal of Education for Teaching*, 20(1), 97-112.

Hankes and Elaine Judith (1996). Investigating the Correspondence Between Native American Pedagogy and Constructivist Based Instruction. Paper Presented at the Annual Convention of the American Educational Research Association, New York.

Hardy and Taylor (1997). Von Glaserfeld's Radical Constructivism. A Critical Review. *Science and Education*, pp. 135-150.

Heeyyoung, C. (2001). A Study of the Consistency Between the Korean National Science Curriculum and Korean Education Programmes for Secondary Science Teachers as to Their Focus on Constructivist Perspectives. *Dissertation Abstracts International*, 62(3), 2001.

Hein, G.E. (1995). The Constructivist Museum. *Journal of Education in Museums*, 16, 21-23.

Henry, C.W. (1995). A Constructivist-based Instructional Approach to Help Fifth-grade Students Improve Selected Elements of Scientific Literacy. *Dissertation Abstracts International,* 57(1), 158-A, 1996.

Herman and William, E. (1995). Humanistic Influences on a Constructivist Approach to Teaching and Learning. Paper Presented at the Annual Meeting of the Association for the Education of Teachers of Science, San Francisco.

Hewson, P.W. and Hewson, M.G. (1983). Effect of Instruction Using Students' Prior Knowledge and Conceptual Change Strategies on Science Learning. *Journal of Research in Science Teaching,* 20, 731-743.

Honebein, P. (1996). Seven Goals for the Design of Constructivist Learning Environments. In B. Wilson, *Constructivist Learning Environments,* pp.1-24. New Jersey: Educational Technology Publications.

Hurst (1994). The Cognitive Nature of Successful Predictive Reasoning in Biology and the Role of Practice in Developing Effective Prediction Problem Solving Skills. *Dissertation Abstracts International,* 55(11), 33465-A, 1995.

Hyang Lim, K. (1995). Science in a Constructivist Classroom: Progress in a Five-year Old Child's Reasoning About Water Dynamics. *Dissertation Abstracts International,* 57(2), 629-A, 1996.

Ibrahim (2001). Examining the Impact of the Guided Constructivist Teaching Method on Students' Misconceptions About Concepts of Newtonian Physics. *Dissertation Abstracts International,* 60(2), 2001.

Illman, T.H. (1998). "Constructivism" and Cooperation Between Scientists and Educators: A Reply to Crowther. *Electronic Journal of Science Education,* 2(3).

Inac, Kang (1995). The Constructivist Principles and the Design of Instruction: A Case Study of An Associate Instructor-Training Programme. *Dissertation Abstracts International,* 56(6), 231-A, 1995.

Isbell and Kelly Jeanne (1999). Developing a Student's Sense of Self: A Constructivist Evaluation of the First Four Years of the International School of the Americas. *Dissertation Abstracts International*, 61(1), 43-A, 2000.

James, D.M. (2000). Pedagogical Perspectives and Implicit Theories of Teaching: First Year Science Teachers Emerging from a Constructivist Science Education Programme. *Dissertation Abstracts International*, 61(10), 3944-A, 2000.

Jonassen, D. (1991). Objectivism Vs Constructivism. *Educational Technology Research and Development*, 39(3), 5-14.

Jonassen, D.H. et. al. (1993). *Structural Knowledge: Techniques for Representing, Conveying and Acquiring Structural Knowledge*, Hillsdale, NJ: Eribaum.

Joseph, J.A. (2000). A Qualitative Study of the Beliefs and Practices of a Group of Effective Middle School Teachers with Respect to Constructivist Learning and Teaching Environments. *Dissertation Abstracts International*, 61(11), 4276-A, 2001.

Kala, L. (2001). History and Philosophy of Science. Cognitive Science and Science Education. *Indian Educational Review*, 37(2), 3-21.

Kant (1983). Philosophy of Constructivism. In *Constructivism in Education*. (ed.). by L.P. Steffe and J.Gale, Lawrence Erlbaum Associates (1995), 3-15.

Kaur, Amandeep (2004). Constructivism. Paper Presented at 17th Annual Conference of All India Association for Educational Research as International Conference on Fourth Wave Education, Saurashtra University, Rajkot. Jan. 10-12.

Keeves, J.P. (ed.). (1997). *Educational Research, Methodology and Measurement: An International Handbook*. Cambridge: Cambridge University Press.

Kemeny, G. (1963). *A Philosopher Looks at Science*, New Jersey: Van Nostrand Company, Inc., Princeton.

Kerlinger, F.N. (1983). *Foundations of Behavioural Research*. New Delhi: Surjeet Publications.

Kilpatrick, J. (1987). What Constructivism Might be in Mathematics Education? In Proceedings of PME XI, Montreal.

Kilpatrick, W.H. (1919). *The Project Method*. New York: Teachers College Press.

Kim, B.J. (1994). The Use of Mnemonics in Constructivist Teaching. *Dissertation Abstracts International*, 55(8), 150-A, 1995.

Kimball, M.L. (1967-68). Understanding the Nature of Science: A Comparison of Scientists and Science Teachers. *Journal of Research in Science Teaching*, 5(2), 110-120.

King, Alison (1994). Guiding Knowledge Construction in the Classroom: Effects of Teaching Children How to Question and How to Explain. *American Educational Research Journal*, 31(2), 338-368.

King, M. (ed.). (1995). Studies in Science Education. A Publication of Science, Mathematics and Information Technology in Education, Research Unit, Faculty of Education. University of Sydney, Vol. 1.

Klopfer, L.E. and Cooley, W.W. (1963). The History of Science Cases for High Schools in the Development of Student Understanding of Science and Scientists. *Journal of Research in Science Teaching*, 1(1), 33-47.

Kretchmer, David. (1995). Students' Understanding of Plant Structure-Function Relationships: A Constructivist-Social Constructivist View. *Dissertation Abstracts International*, 56(12), 4715-A, 1996.

Kuhn Thomas (1970). *The Structure of Scientific Revolutions*. Chicago, University of Chicago.

Kurth, L.A., et. al. (2001). The Case of Carla: Dilemmas of Helping All Students to Understand Science. *Science Education*, 86(3), 287-313.

Kuslan, L.I. and Stone, A.H. (1968). *Teaching Children Science: An Inquiry Approach*. California: Wadsworth Publishing Company, Inc.

Laforgia, Joseph (1988). The Affective Domain Related to Science Education and Its Evaluation. *Science Education*, 72(4), 407-421.

Lamar, T.P. (2001). Students' Perceptions of Constructivist Pedagogy. *Dissertation Abstracts International*, 62(3), 906-A. 2001.

Larochelle, M.; Bednarz, N. and Garrison, J. (Ed). (1998). *Constructivism and Education*. Cambridge: Cambridge University Press.

Layton, David (ed.) (1990). *Innovations in Science and Technology Education*. Belgium: UNESCO. Imprimerie Duculot.

Leach, J. (2002). Teachers' Views on the Future of the Secondary Science Curriculum. *School Science Review*, 83(304), 43-50.

Lebow, D. (1993). Constructivist Values for Instructional Design: Five Principles Toward a New Mindset. Educational Technology Research and Development, 41(3), 4-16.

Lederman, N.G. and Druger, Marvin (1985). Classroom Factors Related to Changes in Student's Conceptions of the Nature of Science. *Journal of Research in Science Teaching*, 22(7), 649-662.

Lederman, N.G. and O'Malley, M. (1990). Students' Perceptions of Tentativeness in Science: Development, Use and Sources of Change. *Science Education*, 74, 225-239.

Lerman (1989). Constructivism, Mathematics and Mathematics Education. *Education Studies in Mathematics*, 20, 211-223.

Levin, Diane E. (1996). Endangered Play, Endangered Development: A Constructivist View of the Role of Play in Development and Learning. *ERIC Document Reproduction Service*, ED405104.

Levitt, K.E. (2002). An Analysis of Elementary Teachers' Beliefs Regarding the Teaching and Learning of Science. *Science Education*, 86(1), 1-50.

Likert, R. (1932). A Technique for the Measurement of Attitudes. Archieves of Psychology, p. 140.

Lori, A. (1996). Autonomy in a Constructivist Classroom. *Dissertation Abstracts International*, 57(6), 2349-A, 1996.

Louise, S.E. (2000). The Role of a Teacher Study Group in Negotiating Constructivist Science Teaching in An Elementary School. *Dissertation Abstracts International*, 62(1), 121-A, 2001

Lynn Renz, B. (1996). Developing a School Assessment Model from a Constructivist Perspective. *Dissertation Abstracts International*, 57(2), 521-A, 1996.

Lynn, I.K. (1998). Students' Experiences in a Constructivist Classroom. *Dissertation Abstracts International*, 112-A, 1998.

Lyons, Carol A. (1996). Applying Constructivist Principles in Reading Recovery Professional Development Classes: Insights from Seven Hundred Teacher Leaders. *ERIC Document Reproduction Service*, ED450366.

Martin Ralph, et. al. (1998). *Science for All Children. Methods for Constructing Understanding*. Massachusetts: Allyn and Bacon, A Viacom Company.

Matthews, M.R. (1980). 'Knowledge, Action and Power'. In R. Mackie (Ed.) *Literacy and Revolution: The Pedagogy of Paulo Freire*, Pluto Press, London, pp. 82-92.

Matthews, M.R. (1993). Constructivism and Science Education: Some Episte Mological Problems. *Journal of Science Education and Technology*, 2(1), 359-370.

Matthews, M.R. (1994). Discontent with Constructivism. Studies in Science Education, 24, 165-171.

Matthews, M.R. (1995). *Challenging New Zealand Science Education*, Dunmore Press, Palmerston North.

Matthews, M.R. (1997). 'Israel Scheffler on the Role of History and Philosophy of Science in Science Teacher Education', *Studies in Philosophy and Education*, 16 (1-2), 159-173.

Matthews, M.R. (Ed.) (1998). *Constructivism and Science Education: A Philosophical Examination*, Kluwer Academic Publishers, Dordrecht.

Matthews, M.R. (2000). Constructivism in Science and Mathematics Education. In D.C. Phillips (ed.), *National Society for the Study of Education*, 99th Year Book, Chicago, University of Chicago Press.

Mayer, R. (1996). Learners as Information Processors: Legacies and Limitations of Educational Psychology's Second Metaphor. In *Educational Psychologist*, 31, 151-161.

Mc.Donnough and Jacqueline Theresa (2002). Implications of Reported Use of Constructivism with Diverse Populations. *Dissertation Abstracts International.* 63(6), 2141-A, 2002.

Mc.Inerney, D.M. and Mc.Inerney, V. (1999). *Educational Psychology. Constructing Learning.* (2nd edition). Prentice hall.

Meichtry, Yvonne J. (1995). Elementary Science Methods: Strategies to Measure and Develop Student Views About the Nature of Science. Paper Presented at the Annual Meeting of the Association for the Education of Teachers of Science, San Francisco.

Merrill, M.D. (1991). Constructivism and Instructional Design. *Educational Technology*, 31(5), 45-53.

Mertens, D.M. (1998). *Research Methods in Education and Psychology. Integrating Diversity with Quantitative and Qualitative Approaches.* London: Sage Publications, Inc.

Michael James, D. (2001) Pedagogical Perspectives and Implicit Theories of Teaching: First Year Science Teachers Emerging from a Constructivist Science Educational Programme. *Dissertation Abstracts International*, 61(10), 3944-A, 2001.

Michael, P. (2001). Sincerity and Reading: Dilemmas in Constructivism. *Dissertation Abstracts International*, 62(3), 902-A, 2001.

Millar, Robin (1989). *Doing Science: Images of Science in Science Education.* London: Falmer Press.

Millar, R. (1989). Constructive Criticisms. *International Journal of Science Education*, 11, 587-596.

Miller and Seigler, A.C. (1990). Effects of Hands-on Activity-based Science and a Supportive Instructional Environment on At-risk Sixth-Grade Students' Attitude Toward Science, Achievement in Science, Goal Orientation and Cognitive Engagement in Science. *Dissertation Abstracts International*, 52(5), 1703-A, 1991.

Mooney-Frank and Ann Janice (2000). William Heard Kilpatrick: Progressive Educator, Curriculum Innovator and Social Philosopher. The Impact of his Project Method on Today's Innovations. *Dissertation Abstracts International*, 61(10), 3879-A, 2001

Moss, D.M. (2001). Examining Student Conceptions of the Nature of the Science. *International Journal of Science Education*, 23(8), 771-790.

Nagel, E. (1979). *The Structure of Science. Problems in the Logic of Scientific Explanation*. London: Kegan Paul Limited.

National Council of Educational Research and Training (1964). *General Science Handbook of Activities for Classes VI-VIII*. New Delhi: National Printing works.

National Council of Educational Research and Training (1989). *Science. A Textbook for Class VIII*. Mathura: Prabhat Printing Press.

National Council of Educational Research and Training (1997). *Fifth Survey of Educational Research 1988-92, Trend Reports*. Volume I and II.

National Council of Educational Research and Training (2000). *National Curriculum Framework for School Education*. New Delhi: Supreme Offset Printers.

National Council of Educational Research and Training (2005). *National Curriculum Framework for School Education*. New Delhi: Supreme Offset Printers.

National Research Council (1996). *National Science Education Standards*. Washington, DC: National Academy Press.

National Research Council (NRC). (2000). *Inquiry and the National Science Education Standards: A Guide for Teaching and Learning.* Washington, D.C.: National Academy Press.

Neathery, M.F. (1992). Elementary and Secondary Students' Perceptions Towards Science: Correlations with Gender, Ethnicity, Ability, Grade and Science Achievement. *Journal of Research in Science Teaching,* 22, 347-358.

Noll, Victor H. (1942). *The Teaching of Science in Elementary and Secondary Schools.* New York: Longmans, Green & Co.

Noll, V.H. (1965). *Introduction of Educational Measurement.* Boston: Houghton Mifflin.

Novak, J. D. (2002). Meaningful Learning: The Essential Factor for Conceptual Change in Limited or Inappropriate Prepositional Hierarchies Leading to Empowerment of Learners. *Science Education,* 86 (4), 548-571.

Novak, J.D. and Gowin, D.B. (1984). *Learning How to Learn.* New York: Cambridge University Press.

Nuffield 11-13 (1986). *How Scientists Work, How Science is Used, Teachers Guides 1&2.* London: Longman, Green and Co.

Obsorne, R.J. and Wittrock, M.C. (1983). Learning Science: A Generative Process. *Science Education,* 67(4), 489-508.

Osborn, J. (1997). Constructivist Metaphors of Learning Science. *Science and Education,* 6, 121-133.

Osborne, J.F. (1996). Beyond Constructivism. *Science Education,* 80(1), 53-82.

Palas Denise D. (2002). Qualities of Interactions Between Constructivist – in Formed Elementary Mentor Teachers and Their Student Teachers. *Dissertation Abstracts International,* 62(3), 2141-A, 2002.

Papert, S.A. (1991). Situating Constructionism. In I. Harel and S. Papert (ed.), *Constructionism.* Pp. (1-12). Norwood, NJ: Ablex.

Pena-p'erez and Judith Beatriz (2000). Participation, Interaction and Meaning Construction in a University Level Course Using Computer Bulletin Board As A Supplement to Regular Class Discussion. *Dissertation Abstracts International,* 61(1), 85-A, 2000.

Philips, D.C. (2000). *Constructivism in Education: Opinions and Second Opinions on Controversial Issues.* National Society for the Study of Education, Chicago.

Phillips, D.C. (1995). The Good, the Bad and the Ugly: The Many Faces of Constructivism. *Educational Researcher,* 24(7), 5-12.

Piaget, J. (1926). *The Language and Thought of the Child.* Routledge & Kegan Paul Limited, New York.

Piaget, J. (1951). *Judgement and Reasoning in the Child.* London: Routledge & Kegan Paul Limited.

Piaget, J. (1951). *The Child Conception of Physical Causality.* New York: Routledge & Kegan Paul Limited.

Piaget, J. (1973). *To Understand is to Invent: The Future of Education.* New York: Grossman Publishers.

Piaget, J. and Inhelder (1971). *Mental Imagery in the Child.* New York: Routledge & Kegan Paul Limited.

Pooran, L. (2000). A Comparison of the Effects of Social Constructivist and Traditional Approaches to Teaching on Students' Attitude and Achievement in High School Chemistry. *Dissertation Abstracts International,* 61(7), 2578-A, 2001.

Popham, W.J. (1981). *Measuring Educational Achievement.* New Delhi: Prentice Hall of India Private Limited.

Popper, K.R. (1959). *The Logic of Scientific Discovery.* London: Hutchinson.

Posner (1982). Accommodation of Scientific Conception: Towards a Theory of Conceptual Change. *Science Education,* 66(2), 211-227.

Preece, P.F.W.. and Baxter, J.H. (2000). The Superstitious and Pseudo-beliefs of Students, *International Journal of Science Education,* 22(11), 1147-1156.

Presseisen, Barbara Z. and Beyer, Francine S. (1994). Facing History and Ourselves: An Instructional Tool for Constructivist Theory. Paper Presented at Annual Meeting of the American Educational Research Association, New Orleans.

Rao Manjula (2006) Relevance of Upanishads to Value Education, Unpublished ERIC Project, NCERT.

Resnick, L.B. (1987). Learning in School and Out. *Educational Researcher,* 16, 13-20.

Reynolds, T.H. (1995). Addressing Gender and Cognitive Issues in the Mathematics Classroom: A Constructivist Approach. *ERIC Document Reproduction Service,* ED404183.

Richmond, G. and Striley, J. (1996). Making Meaning in Classroom: Social Processes in Small-group Discourse and Scientific Knowledge Building. *Journal of Research in Science Teaching,* 33(8), 839-858.

Roger, G.C. (1999). Comparison of Student Learning About Diffusion and Osmosis in Constructivist and Traditional Classrooms. *International Journal of Science Education,* 21(6), 687-698.

Roney, W.D. (1968). *Inquiry Techniques for Teaching Science.* New Delhi: Prentice Hall.

Roth, W.M. and Lucas, K.B. (1997) From "Truth" to "Invented reality'. A Discourse Analysis of High School Physics Student's Talk About Scientific Knowledge. *Journal of Research in Science Teaching,* 34, 145-180.

Rubba, P. and Anderson, H. (1978). Development of An Instrument to Assess Secondary Students' Understanding of Nature of Scientific Knowledge. *Science Education,* 62(4), 449-458.

Russo, et. al., (1995). Thinking About Thinking: A Constructivist Approach to Critical Thinking in the College Curriculum. *ERIC Document Reproduction Service,* ED390353.

Sahlstrom, F. and Lindblad (1998). Subtexts in the Science Classroom-An Exploration of the Social Construction of Science Lessons and School Careers. *Learning and Instruction,* 8(3), 195-214.

Saleska, Thomas John (2000). A Study of the Constructivist Teaching Behaviours within a Population of Elementary Science Teachers. *Dissertation Abstracts International,* 61(11), 4329-A, 2001.

Salim, D.K. (1997). The Influence of the Guided Constructivist Instructional Model on Attitudes Toward Secondary-level Physics. *Dissertation Abstracts International*, 58(8), 3070-A, 1998.

Salomon, G. and Perkins, D. (1998). Individual and Social Aspects of Learning In: P. Pearson and A. Iran – Nejad (Eds.) *Review of Research in Education*, 23, Washington, DC. American Education Research Association.

Sang-chong, L. (1997). Teacher Understanding of the Nature of Science and Its Impact on Student Learning About the Nature of Science in STS/Constructivist Classrooms. *Dissertation Abstracts International*, 58(8), 3072-A, 1998.

Sarangapani, P.M. (1999). Piaget's Theory Going Back in Order to go Forward. *Indian Educational Review*, 35(2), 1-23.

Saunders, W.L. (1992). The Constructivist Perspective: Implications and Teaching Strategies for Science. *School Science and Mathematics*, 92(3), 136-141.

Schaverien Lynette (1999). A Biological Basis for Generative Learning in Technology-and-Science Part I: A Theory of Learning. *International Journal of Science Education*, 21(12), 1223-1235.

Science: Curriculum-Resource-Handbook. *A Practical Guide for K-12 Science Curriculum*. (1992). California: Kraus International Publications Corwin Press.

Scott, Phillip (1987). A Constructivist View of Learning and Teaching in Science. Childrens Learning in Science Project. *Centre for Studies in Science and Maths Education*. University of Leeds, England U.K.

Scricco, et. al. (2000). The Use of Technology in the Modern Foreign Language Classroom. A Constructivist Approach Using a Secondary School Test Case. *Dissertation Abstracts International*, 62(1), 2001.

Sears, J. and Sorensen, P. (2000). *Issues in Science Teaching*. London: Falmer Press.

Senapathy, H.K. (2004). Integrating Digital Technology into Constructivist Learning Environment. Paper Presented at 17th Annual Conference of All India Association for Educational Research as International Conference on Fourth Wave Education, Saurashtra University, Rajkot. Jan. 10-12.

Shah, D.B. (2004). Constructivism a Paradigm and Classroom Learning. Paper Presented at 17th Annual Conference of All India Association for Educational Research as International Conference on Fourth Wave Education, Saurashtra University, Rajkot. Jan. 10-12.

Sharma, H.L. (1989). *School Science Education in India.* New Delhi: Commonwealth Publishers.

Sherri, A. (1995). The Effects of a Constructivist-Learning Environment on Student Cognition of Mechanics and Attitude Towards Science: A Case Study. *Dissertation Abstracts International,* 56(8), 2981-A, 1996

Shon, Minho. (2001). Why Educational Reform Persists: A Study on Routine Grounds of Classroom Lessons in the Korean Case. *Dissertation Abstracts International,* 62(11), 3680-A, 2002.

Shrivastava, S.P. and Shrivastava, M. (2004). Approaches to Education: Constructivism. Paper Presented at 17th Annual Conference of All India Association for Educational Research as International Conference on Fourth Wave Education, Saurashtra University, Rajkot. Jan. 10-12.

Shuell, T.J. (1990). Phases of Meaningful Learning. *Review of Educational Research,* 60(4), 531-547.

Shymansky, J.A., Yore. L.D., Treatgust, D.T., Thiele, R.B., Harrison, A., Waldrys, B.G., Stockmayer, S.M. and Venville, G. (1997). Examining the Constructivism Process: A Study of Changes in Level 10 Students Understanding of Classical Mechanics. *Journal of Research in Science Teaching,* 34, 571-593.

Shymansky, James A., Yore, Larry D. and Anderson, John O. (2000). A Study of Changes in Students Science Attitudes, Awareness and Achievement Across Three Years As a Function of the Level of Implementation of Interactive-constructivist Teaching Strategies Promoted in a Local Systemic Effort. *ERIC Document Reproduction Service:* No. ED439954.

Simon, M. (1995). Elaborating Models of Mathematics Teaching: A Response to Steffe and Ambriossio. *Journal of Research in Mathematics Education*, 26(2), 160-162.

Smith, V.C. and Jones, W.E. (1959). *Science for Modern Living*. New York: J.B. Lippincott Company.

Solomon, J. (1994). The Rise and Fall of Constructivism. *Studies in Science Education*, 23, 1-19.

Songer, N.B. and Linn, M.C. (1991). How do Students' Views of Science Influence Knowledge Integration? *Journal of Research in Science Teaching*, 28(9), 761-784.

Sood, J.K. (1964). An Investigation into the Understanding of the Nature of Science Among the National Science Talent Search Awardees, Science Teachers and the Non-selected NSTS Students. *Indian Educational Review*, 13(4), 138-143.

Sook, J.M. (2001). A Case Study of Middle School Teachers' Pedagogical Beliefs and Practices in Constructivist Approach Doing Web Based Projects. *Dissertation Abstracts International*, 62(7), 2001.

Speering,W. and Rennie, L. (1996). Students' Perceptions about Science: The Impact of Transition from Primary to Secondary School. Research in Science Education, 26, 283-298.

Staver, J.R. (1998). Constructivism: Sound Theory for Explicating the Practice of Science and Science Teaching. *Journal of Research in Science Teaching*, 35(5), 501-520.

Steffe, C.P. and D'Ambrosio, B.S. (1995). Towards a Working Model of Constructivist Teaching. A Reaction to Simon. *Journal of Research in Mathematics Education*, 26, 146-159.

Steffe, L.P. and J. Gale (ed.). (1995). *Constructivism in Education*. Hillsdale, NJ: Lawrence Erlbaum.

Stevens, T. (2004). Constructivism & Behaviorism and Their Construction to Education. Paper Presented at 17th Annual Conference of All India Association for Educational Research as International Conference on Fourth Wave Education, Saurashtra University, Rajkot. Jan. 10-12.

Stofflett, R.T. (1998). Putting Constructivist Teaching into Practice in Undergraduate Introductory Science. *Electronic Journal of Science Education*, 3(2).

Susan, M.H. (1999). Science Conceptions and Connections: How Third Graders Engage in Inquiry to Learn Science. *Dissertation Abstracts International*, 60(3), 694-A, 1999.

Sutton, C.R. and Haysom, J.T. (1974). *Science Teacher Education Project. The Art of the Science Teacher.* London: Mc. Grawhill Book Company (U.K.) Limited.

Talwar, P. and Sharma, M. (2004). Result of Mental Construction-Constructivism. Paper Presented at 17th Annual Conference of All India Association for Educational Research as International Conference on Fourth Wave Education, Saurashtra University, Rajkot. Jan. 10-12.

Tannenbaum, R.W. (1968). The Development of Test of Science Processes. *Dissertation Abstracts International*, 29, 2159-A, 1969.

Taylor, P.C. and Fraser, B.J. (1991). CLES: An Instrument for Assessing Constructivist-Learning Environment. A Paper Presented to the National Association for Research in Science Teaching, Fontane, Wisconsin.

Taylor, P.C., Fraser, B.J., and Fisher, D.L. (1997). Monitoring Constructivist Classroom Environments. *International Journal of Educational Research*, 27(4), 293-302.

Theresa, D.M. (2003). Relationship of Constructivist Learning Environment to Student Attitudes and Achievement in High School Mathematics and Science. *Dissertation Abstracts International*, 63(7), 2455-A, 2005.

Thomas, H.D. (1996). Constructivist, Motivation and Achievement: The Impact of Classroom Mathematics Environments and Instructional Programmes. *Dissertation Abstracts International*, 57(4), 1484-A, 1996.

Thorndike, R.L. and Hagen, E. (1960). *Measurement and Evaluation in Psychology & Education.* London: John Wiley and sons Inc.

Thurstone, L.L. and Chave (1929). *The Measurement of Attitude.* Chicago: Chicago University Press.

Tobin, K.G. and Capie, W. (1982). Development and Validation of a Group Test of Integrated Science Processes. *Journal of Research in Science Teaching*, 19(2), 133-141.

Tobin, K. and Dawson, G. (1992). Constraints to Curriculum Reform: Teachers and the Myths of Schooling. *Educational Technology Research and Development*, 40(1), 81-92.

Tobin, K. (ed.). (1993). *The Practice of Constructivism in Science Education*. Washington DC: AAAS Press.

Tsai, C.C. (1997). The Interplay Between Scientific Epistemological Beliefs and Preferences for Constructivist Learning Environments of Taiwanese Eighth Graders. Paper Presented at the Fourth International Seminar 'From Misconceptions to Constructed Understanding', Cornell University, Ithaca, New York.

Tsai, C.C. (1999). The Progression Toward Constructivist Epistemological Views of Science: A Case Study of the STS Instruction of Taiwanese High School Female Students. *International Journal of Science Education*, 21(11), 1201-1222.

Tunnicliffe, S.D. (1981). "What is Science?" *School Science Review*, 62(2), 548-550.

United Nations Educational Scientific and Cultural Organization, (1980). *UNESCO Handbook for Science Teachers*. U.K.: Page Bros. (Norwich) Limited.

Vaidya, N. (1981). *Some Aspects of Piaget's Work and Science Teaching*. New Delhi: S. Chand & Company (Pvt.) Ltd.

Vaidya, N. (1996). *Science Teaching for the 21st Century*. New Delhi: Deep & Deep publications.

Vaidya, N. and Rajput, J.S. (1977). *Reshaping our School Science Education*. New Delhi: IBIT Publishing Company.

Vardhini, V.M. (1983). Development of a Multimedia Instructional Strategy for Teaching Science (Physics and Chemistry) At Secondary Level. Unpublished Ph.D. Thesis, CASE, M.S. University of Baroda.

Varma, V.P. & William, P. (1976). *Piaget, Psychology and Education.* London: Hodden & Stroughton.

Victor, E. and Lerner, M.S. (1971). *Readings in Science Education for the Elementary School* (2nd Edition). New York: The Macmillan Company.

Vijayalakshmi, K.S. (2004). Approaches to Education-Constructivism, Cognitivism, Behaviourism. Paper Presented at 17th Annual Conference of All India Association for Educational Research as International Conference on Fourth Wave Education, Saurashtra University, Rajkot. Jan. 10-12.

Von Glaserfeld E. (1984). An Introduction to Radical Constructivism. In P. Watzlanick (Ed.), *The Invented Reality.* (pp.17-40) New York: Norton.

Von Glaserfeld, E. (1990). *An Exposition of Constructivism Why Some Like It Radical* in Davis, Maher and Noddings (Eds.) Constructivist Views on the Teaching and Learning of Mathematics. JRME Monograph, Reston, Virginia, NCTM.

Von Glaserfeld, E. (1995). A Constructivist Approach to Teaching. In L.Steffe and J.Gale (ed.). *Constructivism in Education.* (pp.3-16). Hillsdale, NJ: Lawrence Erlbaum.

Von Glaserfeld, E. (1996). Footnotes to "The Many Faces of Constructivism". *Educational Researcher,* 25(6), 19-20.

Vosniadou, S. (1996). Towards a Revised Cognitive Psychology Fir New Advances in Learning and Instruction. *Learning and Instruction,* 6, 95-109.

Vygotsky, L. (1978). *Mind in Society* (Ed.) M. Cole et al. Cambridge, MA: Harward University Press.

Wade, H.B. and James P.G. (1994). Scientific Literacy for Decision Making and the Social Construction of Scientific Knowledge. *Science Education,* 78(2), 185-201.

Wallace, J. and Louden, W. (2002). *Dilemmas of Science Teaching. Perspectives on Problems of Practice.* London: Falmer Press.

Watts, M. and Folfili, Z. (1998). Towards Critical Constructivist Teaching. *International Journal of Science Education,* 20(20), 173-185.

Wesche and Martin Volney (2002). Effects of Behaviourist and Constructivist Mathematics Lessons on Upper Elementary Students' Learning About the Area of a Triangle. *Dissertation Abstracts International*, 63(3), 867-A, 2002.

Wheatley, G.H. (1991). Constructivist Perspectives on Science and Mathematics Learning. *Science Education*, 75(1), 9-21.

White and Janet Hatley (1999). Constructivism in a College Biology Classroom: Effects on Content Achievement, Cognitive Growth and Science Attitude to At-risk Students. *Dissertation Abstracts International*, 61(2), 555-A, 2000.

William, F. and Mc.Comas (1999). *The Nature of Science in Science Education: Rationale and Strategies*. Science and Technology Education Library, Kluwer Academic Publishers.

Wilson, B. and Cole, P. (1991). A Review of Cognitive Teaching Models. *Educational Technology Research and Development*, 37(4), 47-64.

Windridge, C. (1966). *Essential Science*. Book Schofield and Sims Limited.

Windschitl, Mark. and Andre, Thomas. (1998). Using Computer Simulations to Enhance Conceptual Change: The Roles of Constructivist Instruction and Student Epistemological Beliefs. *Journal of Research in Science Teaching*, 35(2), 145-160.

Yager, R.E. (1988). A New Focus for School Science. *School Science and Mathematics*, 88(3), 181-190.

Yager, R.E. (1991). The Constructivist Learning Model Towards Real Reform in Science Education. *Science Teacher*, 58, 52-57.

Yager, R.E. (1993). Constructivism and Science Education Reform. *Science Education International*, 4(1), 13-15.

Yager, R.E. (2000). Science Education a Science? *Electronic Journal of Science Education*, 2(1).

Yagnik, M.K. and Likhia, K.S. (2004). Constructivism and Instructional Constructional Considerations in Science Teaching. Paper Presented at 17th Annual Conference of All India Association for Educational Research as International Conference on Fourth Wave Education, Saurashtra University, Rajkot. Jan. 10-12.

Yore, L.D. (2000). Enhancing Science Literacy for All Students with Embedded Reading Instruction and Writing to Learn Activities. Journal of Deaf Studies and Deaf Education, 5, 105-122.

Yore, L.D. (2001). What is Meant by Constructivist Science Teaching and Will the Science Education Community Stay the Course for Meaningful Reform? *Electronic Journal of Science Education*, 5(4), 100-110.

Youngsun, K. (2001). Profile Change in Pre-service Science Teacher's Epistemological and Ontological Beliefs About Constructivist Learning: Implications for Science Teaching and Learning. *Dissertation Abstracts International*, 61(12), 4722-A, 2001.

Yuen, L.L. (2001). Development of Constructivist Behaviours Among Found New Science Teachers Prepared at University of Iowa. *Dissertation Abstracts International*, 62(3), 2001.

Zeidler, D.L., et. al., (2002). Tangled up in Views: Beliefs in the Nature of Science and Responses to Socio-scientific Dilemmas. *Science Education*, 86(3), 343-367.

Zeigler, John F., (2000). Constructivist Views of Teaching and Learning and Supervising Held by Public School Teachers and Their Influence on Student Achievement in Mathematics. *Dissertation Abstracts International*, 61(1), 54-A, 2000.

WEBSITE ADDRESSES ON CONSTRUCTIVISM

AIL 601 Constructivism. Available at *http://www.bamaed.ua.edu/ail601/cconsthtml*

Black, J.B. and Mc. Clintock, R. (1995). An Interpretation Construction Approach to Constructivist Design. Available at *http://www.ilt.columbia.edu/publications/papers/ICON.htr*

Boudourides, M.A.(1998). Constructivism in Education: A Shoppers Guide.Accessible at *http://www.duth.gr/~mboudour/mab/const.html*

Building an Understanding of Constructivism. Available at *http://www.sedl.org/scimath/compass/v01n03/understand.html*

Cobb, T. (1999). Applying Constructivism: A Test for the Learner as Scientist. Available at *http://www.er.uqam.ca/nobel/r21270/cv/Constructivism.html*

Constructivism and Education: A Shopper's Guide. Available at *http://thasos.cc.duth.gr/~mboudour//mab/constr.html*

Constructivism from Philosophy to Practice. Available at *http//www.stemnet.inf.ca/-elmurphy/cle.html*

Constructivism update 1999. Available at *http://www.cwu.edu/~ceps/constadd.html*

Constructivism: Background Knowledge. Available at *http://college.hmco.com/education/station/concept/construct/conback.html*

Constructivism: The theories. Available at *http://curriculum.calstaatela.edu/faculty/psparks/theorists/501const.html*

Constructivist theory. Available at *http://www.oltc.edu.au/cp/04c.html*

Davidson (1995). Education in the Internet linking theory to reality http://www.nap/edu/readingroom/books/tech gap/ [1997 April 4].

Driver, R.A Constructivist's View of Learning and Teaching. In the Course of the Bremen Symposium. www.univie.ac.at?constructivism/EvG/cgi-bin/redirect.cgi?url=133.pd.

Grinnell, F. (1992). Grinnell's Scientific Attitude at *http://www.stat.wisc.edu/other/ethics/grinnell.html*

Hayes, W.A. (1995). Scientific Attitudes. Available at *http://www.riverboathouse.com/dochayes/scithink/wahsat.html*

Kenyon, R.E. (1978). The Nature of Science. Accessible at *http://www.vgenet.net/diogenes/gs/natofsci.html*

Laura Henriques (1997). Constructivist Teaching and Learning. Accessible at *http://www.educ.uvic.ca/depts/snsc/temporary/cnstrct.html*

Lipps, J.H. (1999). This is Science. Available at *http://www.ucmp.berkeley.edu/people/jlipps/science.html*

National Science Education Standards (1996). Science Teaching Standards. Available at *http://bob.nap.edu/readingroom/books/nses/html/3.html*

Project 2061. (1999). Effective Learning and Teaching. Available at *http://www.project2061.org/tools/sfaaol/chap13.html*

Schwartz, J. (2000). Eighteen Thoughts on the Nature of Science. Availableat*http://www.quackwatch.com/01quackeryrelatedtopics/science.html*

Wilson, F.L. (1999). Science and Human Values. Available at *http://www.rit.edu/~flwstv/plato.html*

Index

❑❑❑